Polished

Adding Shine to your Resume, Cover Letter, and Interview Skills

BY

R. Scott Morris
Morris Consulting, LLC
Chicago, 2010

This book is dedicated to all the business professionals who have had to sit through countless interviews and read countless resumes while wishing they could break professional protocol and tell the speaker/writer what they really think!

And to Alex.

Special thanks to Lauren Baker, Robin Charleston, Kathy Comella Sullivan, and Carol Lucido from the University of Chicago Careers in Business program and to all the CCIB students that helped me refine many points in this book.

And to Diane Foote, Jusvin Dhillon, Georgia McGuire, and Karen Stephanie for their editing help and feedback; and Stewie Morris for his excellent work on the cover design.

Morris Consulting, LLC
Chicago, IL
www.PolishedU.com

ISBN: 978-0615348803

Contents

__Introduction__

For all of you who lack experience with the job search process, it has been a growing passion of mine to help you, and job seekers like you, to improve your understanding of what to write, say, and do during your job hunt. This passion started to crystallize when I became involved at the University of Chicago, my alma mater, working with students who were seeking employment in the financial services industry.

What I realized from my involvement with these students was that the techniques they had developed to be successful in academic life were of little help in the job search process. In fact, I would argue that what they need to know to be successful in their job hunt is the antithesis of what they are being taught in class. Specifically, they are learning to think theoretically, to seek truth and to be self-critical and introspective. I am in no way condemning the modern educational system. Quite the opposite, for I am a great fan of a liberal arts education and the development of thoughtful argument and independent thinking. However, when I am reading resumes and cover letters, or interviewing prospective hires to come work on my team, these traits do not get candidates very far. On the contrary, I am looking for real-life experiences, conciseness, attention to detail, organized thought, competitiveness, self-confidence, and salesmanship, none of which is emphasized in most academic environments.

This book is designed to help young job seekers understand what someone in my position is looking for in a job candidate and to teach them to effectively market and present their skill sets.

It should have value to job searchers of all levels and, perhaps, to those on the other side of the hiring process. However, it is written specifically for those first-time job seekers who have their college pedigrees but little else of substance to offer a potential employer. My goal in writing this book is to help you get the most out of what you have and present it in a way that prospective employers will be able to translate into a possible fit with their firm. Hopefully, in the process, you will surprise yourself with how many skills you already possess that are marketable in the business world. With a little polish, we will make these skills easy for prospective employers to see.

I do cover some theoretical constructs, but the book focuses more attention on the "do's and don'ts" of the hiring process. It is intended to help job seekers avoid the common pitfalls (the "don'ts") which will doom their candidacy. The premise is that most people have the raw skills necessary to be successful in their job search; they just need to polish their resumes, cover letters, and interviewing skills (the "do's") to make their skill set shine, and ultimately put them in the best possible position to get the job for which they are best suited.

My qualifications for writing this book are mainly attributed to my many years participating in the recruiting process. I am neither a human resource professional nor a professional recruiter. More important, I would argue, I have been the one who actually makes the hiring decisions. Since I am the one who has had to live directly with the successes and failures of the hiring process, I have developed a keen sense of the individual characteristics and personal traits that lead to job success.

In my twenty years in the financial services industry, even as a senior executive, I have taken an unusually direct role in recruiting. I firmly believe that a well-functioning recruitment process is an integral part of any growing business. While a managing director at Goldman Sachs and a partner at Hull Trading, I was actively involved in the on-campus recruiting process at a number of top-tier schools such as Carnegie Mellon, the University of Chicago, the University of Pennsylvania, and the Massachusetts Institute of Technology. Throughout my career, I have reviewed many thousands of resumes and cover letters and have performed over five hundred first- and second-round interviews.

In addition, over the last three years, I have conducted job skills workshops for undergraduates at the University of Chicago and have personally mentored many of these students in their job searches. In fact, many of the examples in this book are derived from my experience working with these students.

This book represents my views and observations, and though I believe these to be widely supported by other professionals in the business community, some may disagree. This, unfortunately, is one of the biggest problems that all first-time job seekers face. There are no laws or undisputed truths that can be applied to determine the likelihood of a successful hire. In the end, the hiring process is highly subjective. There are only personal judgments and imperfect heuristics, which may differ widely from one human resource professional or decision maker to another. I believe I can enlighten you, the job seeker, about potential imperfections and help you position yourself for success, but there will always be a fair amount of uncertainty and luck involved in the process.

The outline of this book is quite straightforward. First, I will address some of the key philosophical/theoretical points which have overall importance to the recruiting process. I start with a visit to the Oracle of Delphi (Chapter I) to learn about the tenets "Know Thyself" and "Nothing in Excess." Next, I describe the recruiting process from the perspective of a recruiter (Chapters II and III) before I delve headfirst into the "do's and don'ts" of adding polish to your cover letter (Chapter IV), resume (Chapter V) and interview skills (Chapter VI). These sections are rich with real-life experiences. Finally, I conclude with personal observations about the job search process, such as the importance of corporate culture, and the advantages of small firms versus large firms (Chapter VII). Getting the job is only the first step! It is even better if you start your career off in the right direction.

Let's get started…

I.   **The Oracle of Delphi**

The Oracle of Delphi was viewed by the ancient Greeks as a temple of great wisdom and was often consulted by the Greek rulers before they would make an important military or political move. The head priestess of the Oracle was renowned for predicting the future, but would often prognosticate in riddles that often had more than one plausible interpretation!

The significance of the Oracle here is not to teach you how to predict the future or to talk in riddles. The latter would be most disastrous in an interview. In fact, I will espouse the opposite and implore you throughout this book to write and speak concisely with easy-to-interpret phrases and expressions.

We are most interested in the Oracle's teachings about self-awareness. According to Plato, a visit to the Oracle was a major source of influence on young Socrates and enlightened him to how much he did not know about himself. It is for this same self-awareness that we wish to revisit the Oracle. Specifically, we will explore two important mantras of the teachings of the Oracle: "Know Thyself" and "Nothing in Excess."

These two concepts are quite simple but very powerful. Unfortunately, in my experience, job seekers rarely follow them. I doubt that the concept of a resume and cover letter was even developed at the time of the Oracle (perhaps interviews in some form were, but no matter). Understanding and implementing a strategy that follows these two tenets of the Oracle of Delphi is the most important advice I can give you to separate yourself from the crowd and land that coveted job you seek.

Let's take a look at each of these tenets in more detail.

Know Thyself: Exploring Your Passions

"Knowing Thyself" is understanding what makes you tick. What are your strengths and weaknesses? It involves going to your very core: your passions as well as your limitations. Your resume and cover letter should be a full expression of your passions. If your job search is done properly, it will effectively match you with an opportunity that allows you to express these passions. Expression of your passions will lead to intellectual stimulation, self-satisfaction, energy, and focus in your work. Success is not guaranteed, but the right career fit makes it much more likely.

What are your passions? Sadly, most people have not asked themselves this question. In fact, I would argue that most people do not even know what a passion is. Often when asked about their passions, people will respond in the form of "likes": "I 'like' the financial markets" or "I 'like' math." Therefore, they describe their passions as "the financial market" or "math." These responses do not go deep enough. These are simply expressions of passions, not passions themselves. Passions are more fundamental and sometimes more obtuse. They hit at the core of your being. In an interview, when I hit upon one, the interviewee will get a little tingly inside and her voice will quiver and raise an octave.

To get at your passions, you often have to ask why you like the "likes." Let's take my favorite example of "winning." I have heard many times that someone has a passion for winning. I contend that this is not a passion. It is an expression of one of a few different possible passions. To find the true passion we have to delve a little deeper and ask, "Why do you like to win?" It could be that you like the satisfaction of being the best that you can be and winning is an expression of that. This is an admirable passion and one that will result in a successful hire for me. However, it could be that you like to see the humiliation and pain of those you have beaten. Winning is also an expression of this passion!

As an interviewer, I need to find out which one it is. If you articulate the former and I sense from the passion in your voice and the look in your eyes that you are sincere, then I have reached a core understanding of what makes you tick. I know that you have a good chance of being successful in a high-pressure, competitive environment, and that you will not cheat and break the rules to win at all costs and get me in trouble. I am starting to think about how to convince you to work on my team!

However, if you cannot articulate why you like to win, I don't quite know what to think of you. Certainly, you have done nothing to differentiate yourself from the other 11 people that I will interview for the same position.

Here are some "likes" and possible passions associated with them:

- Math: solving complex problems
- Playing an instrument: jamming with my friends to create a new sound
- Financial markets: thinking on my feet or taking educated risks
- Winning: striving to be the best
- Improv comedy: creative synthesis or thinking on my feet
- Teaching: joy in seeing others learn
- Engineering: building things

To determine your passions, you have to do this exercise yourself. Spend some time thinking about your core motivations. How do you know when you have hit a passion? When you cannot go any deeper; when the answer to the question "Why do you enjoy seeing others learn?" is self-evident and indivisible.

This exercise sounds easy, but there is one big problem: We often lie to ourselves and are not mature enough to dig so deeply into our own souls. Strangely though, we have no problem analyzing others' strengths and weaknesses. This gives us a back door to get at the right result: Ask those close to you for some critical feedback. What do you think I am good at doing? While you are at it, you may want to ask them what you are NOT good at doing. We are even worse at admitting our shortcomings to ourselves. Understanding our passions is very important, but equally important is understanding where we do not excel. Your ultimate goal is to position your career to fuel your passions and minimize your shortcomings. Knowing thyself will allow you to understand and act accordingly.

Exercise: Understanding hubris and your level of self-awareness

To the below ten questions, please give your answer as a 90% confidence interval. A 90% confidence interval is a range in which you are 90% sure that the correct answer falls in between your two answers.

For instance if you were asked to give a 90% confidence interval on my age, you might be a little confused by my grey (it's silver!) hair and my baby face and maybe need to make a wider range, say 38 to 48, to be 90% sure that you were right. If you happen to have glanced at my resume, you may have remembered the year I graduated from college. Given this information, you might feel more confident with your estimate and could tighten your confidence interval to say 42 to 46.

The point of the exercise is not to make the tightest range, but to get as many answers right as possible. If you are 90% confident and have 10 questions, you should get 9 right. Got it? Good luck.

90% Confidence Level for ...	Low	High
1. Population of the city of Chicago (2007)?		
2. All time high of the Nikkei 225 Stock Index of Japan?		
3. Year in which the Nikkei 225 reached its all time high?		
4. Year in which Wolfgang Amadeus Mozart was born?		
5. Current estimate of USSR citizens that died in WWII?		
6. Length of the Nile river in kilometers?		
7. Year the film Buckaroo Banzai Across the 8th Dimension was released?		
8. Grams of sugar in a 12-ounce Coca-Cola?		
9. Number of countries in the United Nations?		
10. Average low temperature in Jackson Hole, Wyo. in June		

Total Correct: _____   (answers at the end of the chapter—don't peek!)

How did you do? If you got 9 or 10 right, you are in the very small minority. In fact, of the hundreds of times that I have given this test only two—yes, TWO people—have scored within the prescribed range.

"Know Thyself" means that we are all overconfident in our ability to judge uncertain outcomes. Overconfidence causes us to say and do stupid things. Keep this in mind later when we discuss job search strategy and risk minimization in your cover letters, resumes, and interviews.

Nothing in Excess

While the previous tenet of the Oracle of Delphi, "Know Thyself," may be philosophical and perhaps a bit spiritual, the second is much more practical. There is a philosophical aspect of "Nothing in Excess" which concerns controlling your ego and using sound, prudent judgment. (See Shakespeare's *Macbeth* for further inspiration on the subject.) However, for this exercise we are going to take a much more narrow definition. "Nothing in Excess" for your job search skills means: Write and say only what needs to be said, not a word or syllable more.

One of the biggest mistakes that most job seekers make is that they do not articulate their key selling points concisely. Perhaps applicants for a senior position can get away with this because they possess a track record of past experience to help differentiate them. However, for a first-time job seeker, there are likely to be many equally qualified candidates competing for every position. You have very little time and space to make a positive, lasting impression. Too many people waste it blabbering about nonsense. Both on your resume and cover letter, as well as during interviews, "Nothing in Excess" means you must learn to be concise. You must learn to answer the question that was asked of you with short, factual statements without superlatives or embellishments, and you must learn to tailor your response to what I, the interviewer or resume reviewer, want to hear, NOT what you think I want to hear.

What do I want to hear? I want to hear how you are going to make my team work better and how you are going to help my business grow. I certainly do not want to hear about all the things that you are going to get out of working for me. We will talk about this in some detail when we discuss cover letters and resumes, but let me state it for the record here. Most would-be employers do not care about what you are going to get out of the experience of working for them. If they do, they will explicitly ask you. Job applicants often make this mistake by wasting precious time and space talking about the value that they will glean from working for me. Nothing loses my attention faster. When I am reviewing job applications, all I care about is what I am going to get from you. Everything that you write and say should reflect this. To paraphrase CEO Kennedy:

Ask not what the firm can do for you, but what you can do for the firm.

This should be the theme of your cover letter and resume.

Finally, "Nothing in Excess" means that your resume and cover letter should not delve into details. The reason that most people write too much in their resumes and cover letters—and talk too much in their interviews—is that they feel that a description of previous tasks and roles is what I want to hear. This may be somewhat true for senior positions where there is likely to be a clear correlation between these tasks and the position for which I am hiring, but for the inexperienced applicants tasks rarely translate. If there are a couple of things you did where the details are important to the job you seek, you can trust that I will ask about them during the interview.

The important take-away is that I want to evaluate the skills that you have learned, not the tasks that you have performed. Skills are general; tasks are detailed. Keep it general and focus on what may be applicable in many job settings.

In sum, the tenor of your message should:

- Contain concise and general statements focused on skills learned rather than tasks performed.
- Include evidence showing how you will add value to the hiring firm.
- Not dwell on what you hope to gain if hired.

Answers: 1) 2.8 million; 2) 38,957.00; 3) 1989; 4) January 27, 1756; 5) 20 million; 6) 6695 kms; 7) 1984; 8) 39; 9) 192; 10) 37 degrees Fahrenheit

II. <u>What Recruiters Are Looking For</u>

The recruiting process has many different variants. I will use as my starting point the most heavily travelled route, and the most structured: the on-campus recruiting process. For monster.com- or headhunter-assisted job searches, there are fewer steps and less structure, but the key insights are the same. Unfortunately, the recruiting process is often very inefficient. It is full of randomness and, sometimes, arbitrary outcomes. We will focus on this issue as well.

Steps in Evaluating a Resume and Cover Letter

Let's step back and think about this. You, the candidate, are supposed to cram everything that is relevant about your possible desirability to a prospective employer into a short cover letter and a one-page resume. These two pages of information then must travel through the postal service or the ether of the Internet. They must then find their way to the right person in the human resources department whose job it is to weed out the list of candidates using their own, sometimes arbitrary, heuristics. If you make this cut, then this person will copy and staple your two pieces of paper and stack them with similar pieces of paper and hand them off to a second- or third-year associate who will be sitting on the other side of the table to judge your fate. These young professionals, your senior by perhaps only a few years, will be using their also somewhat arbitrary heuristics to determine your fit in the organization. Moreover, they will within the first couple of minutes of meeting you—perhaps even before they ask the first question—assess whether or not you have the "stuff" it takes to work at their firm.

I could go on (and will do so shortly), but I don't want to come across as cynical. That is not my goal in this chapter. It is quite the contrary. My goal is to educate you about the recruiting process so that you will not get discouraged. There are many uncontrollable consequences in the job search process, especially for those freshly minted BAs looking for those coveted jobs in the financial services sector. The goal of this book is to give you an edge over the competition, but there is only so much you can control. So don't fret about it and don't get discouraged over what you cannot control. Like anything in life, if you try your best and work at it, you can achieve your goal, but you have to have a strategy and understand what you are up against.

So what can you do to make your cover letter and resume stand out? To minimize the randomness and arbitrariness of the process? We will get to that in a bit. We still have some important groundwork to cover. The first place to start is to give you a little bit more insight on the recruiting process as I remember it at Goldman Sachs.

At some time before I am to come to your campus to meet with you and your fellow students, I receive a stack of resumes and cover letters from your campus recruiting office. It is my task to choose 12 or so candidates to call in for a first-round interview. Perhaps there will be two or three of us interviewing in tandem, but either way the process would be the same. In general, there will be at least twice as many applicants as interview spots. How do I make the cut?

Well, the first key insight in the selection process is that my initial thoughts are not about looking for reasons to select candidates. I am much more focused on winnowing the list at this point. Not until step 3, below, will I start to think about including people:

Step 1: Exclude those with missing information. This is pretty basic. If I specifically ask for a cover letter and one is not submitted, you will not make the cut. Likewise, if your cover letter does not tell me for what job you are applying, it may get lost in the shuffle.

Step 2: 30-second scan of resume. At this stage, I am aggressively looking for people to weed out. If you have a typo or two, you are probably out. If there is no GPA listed, you definitely go in the maybe column and might be excluded outright if I have a large quantity of applicants. Organization of the resume is very important. If it is difficult to read, and/or too wordy, it will make a strong negative impression. Lack of evidence of experience or interest in the particular job I am hiring for is a killer.

Step 3: Perusal. Now you, and positive aspects of your resume and cover letter, matter somewhat. I always start with the cover letter. Sometimes I like to give specific instructions in the job posting to see who is really interested in working on my team and willing to spend the extra time to write me an individual letter. For example, I might ask, "In your cover letter please address your most interesting team experience." If I see that you have addressed this issue and have a concise and organized message on both your cover letter and resume, I will probably keep you in consideration.

Step 4: Supporting evidence. Finally, when I am making the final cut of candidates for first-round interviews, I look for three overriding characteristics:

1. Character traits and skills that are consistent with success.
2. Evidence of a high capacity to learn and grow as your experience grows.
3. Fit with the job description. This has two components:
   - Evidence of a true interest in the nature of the business in question.
   - Skills that will be useful in fulfilling the previous two items.

The next chapter will go into these three topics in much greater detail.

Risk Minimization

I can't emphasize enough how important it is to not give a recruiter a reason to eliminate your resume and cover letter. I call this concept "risk minimization." Like modern portfolio theory, your goal is to construct the resume and cover letter that has the lowest risk-to-reward ratio. You need to develop your message in a way that will be offensive to the fewest number of people. Every word that you add—or detail that you deliver—can be a source of risk and it can derail your application. Remember, when I am looking for a summer intern or a first-year analyst, I am staring at a pool of candidates who all have very similar credentials; at this point your goal should be to avoid being excluded, rather than trying to be chosen. Typos, irrelevant information, sloppy formatting, font size so small that it hurts my eyes, embellishments, and unsupported superlatives are all things that add risk to your chances without yielding any return. Don't worry. I will help you clean up and polish your resume and cover letter and give you some useful risk minimization tools for your interviews as well. We are almost there.

III. Character, Capacity, and Corporate Fit

These concepts are essential in a successful job search process, and in fact, hiring for character and capacity is a fundamental tenet of most well-run organizations. So what are character, capacity, and corporate fit and why are they so important?

Character

Character, in this context, consists of the traits that are commonly found in successful people. Some are universal, such as good judgment, while others are specific to a particular industry or a particular role. For instance, in finance and trading in particular, a proven competitiveness in a team setting such as sports is strongly correlated with success. Thus, evidence of competing on a team would be a highly sought-after character trait. Below are some of the aspects of candidates that I have found reveal character traits that are strongly related to career success:

- **Participation in team sports/competitions:** Illustrates ability to work with others under pressure, and demonstrates competitiveness.

- **Multi-tasking/multiple interests:** Shows the ability to juggle many things at once. Usually, this trait is associated with individuals who do not need a lot of supervision and will find additional, productive things to occupy their time.

- **Enjoyment in new challenges/overcoming hardships:** Shows experience operating outside one's comfort zone.

- **Overachieving:** Most overachievers overachieve in all aspects of their lives. Evidence of this trait in one area is highly correlated to others.

- **Good judgment:** Often a sign of a mature, self-confident individual.

- **Courage to follow one's passions:** This in some situations could be an issue, but in general having a little independence and following what you believe in is a good thing.

- **Risk taking:** Risk taking is a part of life and is necessary for an individual to advance at a firm. It is also how many of us learn right from wrong. Successful people are not afraid to stick their necks out once in a while.

When I am reviewing resumes and cover letters and interviewing job candidates, I am looking for evidence of these traits. Surprisingly, most job applicants make this hard for me. For whatever reasons, they tend to focus on adding details about tasks, saying "I did this and did that," to their resumes and cover letters. Instead, these documents should be teeming with examples of candidates' strongest character traits.

Capacity

Having the right character is important for someone to fit into a particular culture. Having the capacity to grow is essential for that individual to manage the challenges that will face her as she moves up the corporate ladder. Innate intelligence helps, but it is by far not the only driver. There are some people who have a passion for continued self-improvement and a comfort with trying new things. Anyone with a little effort can improve in this area. Here are some examples showing what I mean by "capacity":

- **Evidence of continual learning:** Continual learners take classes because they want to learn, not because of the grade they will receive. They will learn and grow in their careers in ways the grade-conscious individual cannot.

- **Evidence of serious intellectual pursuit:** It's significant when someone has explored in great detail one particular pursuit, going beyond what is asked to become an expert in a subject of interest.

- **Evidence of unbounded creativity:** Creative people are often so in all aspects of their lives, so evidence of creativity in music, improv comedy, or academic research is often correlated to creativity in their careers.

- **Broad knowledge base:** The more you know, the more you will be able to draw from additional areas to create better solutions to the problems you face in your career. Buckaroo Banzai, the pop culture figure of the mid-80s, was a nuclear physicist, neuro-surgeon, race car driver, and rock musician. This broad knowledge base helped him save the world by defeating a band of 8th dimension aliens called Red Lectroids from Planet 10!

Just as I screen for character traits, I also look for capacity in resumes and cover letters, and tailor my interview questions to probe for individuals with a high capacity. Most of the resumes and cover letters that I see don't know how to reflect this. If you have a double major, don't hide it. If you went to science camp to learn more about molecular chemistry, I want to know this. If you spent your break in Quebec fine-tuning your French, work this into your resume. I call these things "hooks." It's a fishing analogy. They "hook" the resume reviewer or interviewer and "reel" them in toward your strong character traits and evidence of high capacity.

Character and capacity are so important to success in a dynamic work environment because the fundamental building blocks of a successful, growing organization are teams. Well-run organizations are constantly dismantling and reorganizing new teams to manage the demands of a changing competitive landscape. People who lack the necessary character traits do not function well in this environment. They need continual oversight from management. They are what we call "high-maintenance" employees.

Likewise, individuals with a low capacity for growth will never be able to develop the creative synthesis necessary to evolve into the future leaders that a growing organization needs to continue its success. They will always be looking to others to tell them what to do. Ignoring capacity in the hiring process could create an organization rife with smart followers. For most organizations, this is a recipe for stagnation.

Corporate Fit

Before we get to the specifics of the recruiting process, let me introduce one more concept that is an important factor in the decision-making process for a firm seeking new employees: Employers are looking for both career and cultural "fit."

The term "fit" is a vague description because it deals with non-measureable attributes of individuals, some of which may be difficult for recruiters to articulate. It may be hard to describe exactly, but employers know it when they see it. In essence, "fit" means that the individual shares the same core values that the firm does. It might not be obvious to someone who has not been exposed to multiple corporate cultures, but there are big differences in the core values of different firms. Some are highly ethical and straight-laced; others are risk-takers and opportunistic. Some value the team over the individual; others value individual initiative and leadership. Some pride themselves in their decentralized management structure; others are militaristic with strict command and control structures. The point is that every corporate culture has its unique set of mores. Success in a particular firm is often dictated by how employees' personality traits "fit" with these mores. It is not just your skills that are being analyzed in the resume and interviewing process, it is also your "fit" in the corporate culture.

This is an important fact to remember and a reason why you as a job seeker need a wide net in choosing your job search strategy. If you are highly ethical and straight-laced and you work at a firm that values risk-takers and opportunists, others, not you, will be the ones who are highly valued and who will move up the corporate ladder. You will be miserable and will feel lost and discouraged.

The moral of the story is to know yourself and be honest in the job application process. Let the free market work and look for the right "fit." Don't be fooled into making a poor career choice if the fit is not right. You will be better off in the long term if the opportunity fits your passions and the firm has the same core values as you. Don't choose Wall Street over Main Street if Main Street is a better fit.

Polish

In our earlier discussion, we spoke about high-level theoretical constructs. The philosophies of the Oracle of Delphi and the importance of character and capacity and corporate fit are all very important concepts, but they are not going to directly help you prepare for on-campus recruiting season or get you noticed by that top-notch consulting firm you have your eyes on. These next two parts of the book are designed to give your job search a step forward by adding some "polish." Polish will help you differentiate yourself from the competition and win that coveted position in the management training program that will start your career in the right direction.

There is no panacea to this process. No golden rule. There are only a number of useful suggestions that I have come across in my years actively recruiting people like you.

These are my observations that I believe are supported by many in the industry, but others may disagree with some of the advice I have to offer. This only again highlights the inefficiencies of the process and the biases that we hiring decision-makers all have.

So let's get going. Let's add a little shine to your job search skills…

IV. Cover Letters

When I am seriously evaluating the credentials of prospective hires, I almost always start with the cover letter. In a cover letter, candidates must convey to me why I should hire them. They must analyze data about themselves and present an organized argument to support these data. In some instances, I may ask them to detail a specific quality or job specification. This is much harder than organizing facts on a resume. It is much more, well, work-like! Because of this, a job seeker's cover letter is a better reflection of his or her interest in working for me and sheds more light on whether he or she has the character and capacity to fit in with my team.

A well-written cover letter can be time-consuming to compose. It must articulate a candidate's interest in a position and a firm. But don't overdo it. More words are seldom the best course of action. Remember the concept of risk minimization and the teachings of the Oracle. Too many words can obscure the nuggets of valuable information a job applicant must convey to a recruiter.

Key Points

Use correct grammar and a readable style. Let's start with the basics. Few of us have sufficient command of the English language to expect to be able to write a cover letter (or resume) without a third party, or two, to proof-read our work. Typos and grammatical errors are a death sentence for your chances. Remember, I, as the cover letter reviewer, have a whole bunch of resumes and cover letters that look very similar, and my first task is to weed out the definite "Nos." A missing punctuation mark, misspelled word, or wrong verb tense makes it easy for me to eliminate you. Am I really that strict? Yes, generally. A candidate has to be something special for me to let one grammatical error slip by. Two and you are dead—especially for those of you who insist on telling me that you have "excellent" communication skills or that you are detail-oriented. You have violated the cardinal rule of the Oracle—"Know Thyself."

Grammatical errors show a sense of laziness and a lack of attention to detail. These are character flaws that I don't want on my team. I always tell my junior team members that if they want to play a larger, more challenging role, they must first show excellence in the smaller, less important tasks. People who understand this understand that excellence in their cover letters is essential. So don't risk it. Have a couple of people who have good grammar skills look at your cover letter for both content and syntax.

Be concise. An inability to articulate your message concisely is a very bad trait in business. Your goal in a cover letter is to create "hooks" that "reel in" your reader to your passions and that highlight your strong character and capacity. Your audience is going to lose interest if you are too verbose. I am reminded of the famous quote most commonly attributed to Blaise Pascal:

> I have only made this letter rather long because I have not had time to make it shorter. [Je n'ai fait celle-ci plus longue que parceque je n'ai pas eu le loisir de la faire plus courte.] (Blaise Pascal, "Lettres provinciales, 16, Dec. 14, 1656," *Cassell's Book of Quotations*, London, 1912. p.718.)

Communicating your thoughts in a concise way takes time and effort, but it is an indication of strong communication skills. It is also an indication of how important a particular job is to you.

By the way, don't think that making your font smaller is a good proxy for conciseness. That doesn't work. It is the content that is important. As a rule of thumb, 11-point font is the smallest you should go. If I have trouble reading it, I won't.

Tailor your message to the reader. Let me start with a simple axiom to follow that will help you make your cover letter much more effective:

> *Focus your message on telling me how your skills and experiences are going to contribute to improving MY team and helping MY business.*

Far too much time and energy in cover letters are wasted explaining what YOU are going to get out of the experience or why YOU are interested in working for me. Unless it is explicitly asked for, this information is at best irrelevant.

You will be tempted to add filler to your cover letter in this vein, because you will think that it makes your message more well-rounded. Don't do it. Remember, that I have a stack of cover letters to slog through. I am looking for specific details about how you can help my team. Don't dilute your message with details that deviate from this theme.

It is not that employers do not care about the well-being of our employees. Quite the contrary: We want our employees to learn and continue to grow, but there is a time and a place for everything. This is not it.

Minimize risk. Remember, I have a stack of potential candidates who look a lot like you. I first have to weed people out. Here are some "don'ts" that could hurt your chances:

- Don't be too cute. Stick to the facts. Self-deprecating humor, creative prose, philosophical insight, famous quotations, etc. are sources of risk and should be used with extreme caution. Also, use a standard font. Don't **use something too casual or** *flowing to try to differentiate yourself*. I recommend Times New Roman. It conveys seriousness and formality.

- Don't be too specific. Avoid using acronyms and providing too much detail about specific tasks. Keep it general. In most instances, I am looking for general skills. If I care to know the specifics, I'll ask you in the interview.

- Don't point out weaknesses or shortcomings. Focus on your strengths. Framing your arguments to downplay your weaknesses or holes in your skill set is not dishonest. It is good marketing.

- Don't assume you know what I might think is important. Be careful trying to seem smart or professionally savvy. Don't try to answer your own questions about what it means to be successful in a particular field, for example, "The three most important attributes to success in business are…." This is hard to pull off and fraught with risk for one simple reason: Not everyone who reads your cover letter will agree with your assessment. If you must add Socratic dialogue, it is best to frame the question in the third person: "People who I have talked to believe that the three things that make a successful consultant are x, y, and z…." This way I cannot fault you for being misinformed. But you are probably not helping your case much. Best to avoid the risk.

- Don't embellish. Avoid words like "excellent," "expert," "extensive knowledge of," "best," or "superior…" UNLESS you can back them up. RISK, RISK, RISK! Guess what happened to the guy who had a typo in the same sentence with the words, "excellent communication skills, both oral and written…"

- Don't try to make your summer or entry-level jobs sound more important than they actually were. Statements like, "advised the CEO" or "developed a comprehensive marketing plan" are great if they are true, but if they are a stretch, you just lost me on ethical grounds.

More on Risk Taking

Before we get into some details about what a good (and bad) cover letter look like, let me take a minute to clarify a little bit about risk taking. In general, risk taking is a good thing. As a business leader, I am looking for people who are willing to take educated risks. In fact, taking appropriate risk is a sign of good judgment and maturity. It is an important piece of the "right" character. However, good judgment in risk taking is defined by weighing the outcomes and maximizing the probability of success. Generally, risk taking on a cover letter shows bad judgment because the candidate has no way of judging the potential outcomes. It is a gamble and the odds are stacked against you. Later, I will highlight a couple of instances when appropriate risks can have potential high rewards, but these instances are few and fit only limited circumstances. As a general rule, evidence of appropriate risk taking *in* your cover letter is good, but risk taking *on* your cover letter itself is bad.

Outline of a Successful Cover Letter

There is not one definitive form for a cover letter, but below is a useful outline that will help keep you on track and focused on writing a concise letter.

For starters, your cover letter should never be longer than one page. The only possible exception is if the job description asks for highly specific details or specifically asks for an essay-like response. Some nonprofit or educational internships are like that. In general, your cover letter should be limited to three or four concise paragraphs.

> **First section (introduction):** This should be one short paragraph that focuses on details to help the reviewer know which pile to put your resume in. It should include simple facts such as:
>
> - Who you are
>
> - What position you are applying for
>
> - Perhaps, how you heard about the position
>
> - Other logistics: timing, where you are coming from such as a school or career fair, etc.
>
> By the way, I cannot tell you the number of times while I was at Goldman Sachs that I received cover letters from applicants who forgot to cut and paste and wanted me to know how great it would be to work at Morgan Stanley. I am sure that they are right, but from my point of view this is very sloppy and shows a gross lack of attention to detail. I seldom took the risk.
>
> **Second section (body):** This should focus on why I should consider you for the job. It should have evidence and experiences that illustrate your passions and your character and capacity. It is acceptable to split this into two separate paragraphs: one focusing on work experiences and one focusing on leadership and organization and team skills.
>
> It is important to populate this section with skills, not tasks; skills are more likely to be portable from one experience to another, but tasks in general are not. For example, say that you had some experience over the summer analyzing some data

in a spreadsheet. It is the analysis and the tools that you used that should be stressed, not the content of the analysis. Read the following two bullets:

Good (task-based):

- Analyzed U.S. Housing Starts data across different states to determine regional differences in economic activity.

Better (skill-based):

- Using Excel macros and Access databases, calculated correlations and standard deviation of U.S. Housing Starts across different states.

Information about *task:* analyzing U.S. Housing Starts is probably not beneficial to my business, but perhaps the *skills:* experience with macros, data management, and statistical analysis are.

What I generally don't want to read:

- Why you think the job to which you are applying will help you reach some goal other than making my team succeed.

  Avoid statements like: "At your firm, I hope to enhance my knowledge of x, y and z."

- Why you think you are smart. I'll determine that.

- How great my company is. I already know that.

  Avoid statements like: "Your firm was recently ranked as the top consulting firm by Consulting Magazine and has an expertise in blah, blah, blah...."

As noted earlier, the singular focus of your cover letter is to illustrate how you will help my team succeed.

Third section (conclusion): Keep it short and sweet. It is okay to re-emphasize a key passion or strong element of your fit. It is also okay to mention a possible personal connection such as a hometown, school, organization, or mutual acquaintance. But the last paragraph is rarely a source of substance; its only real purpose, as in all structured writing, is to provide flow and balance to your letter.

Examples

The best way to understand what a good cover letter looks like is to look at some real examples and see for yourself what works and what does not.

Most of the examples in this book come from my workshops with undergraduates at the University of Chicago Careers in Business program. Mind you that these are all extremely bright individuals. Their errors and transgressions should be a lesson to all of you of just how hard this process can be.

Please read through the example letter below. I will tear it apart, oops, I mean analyze it afterwards in detail.

Example 1: Andrea Maroon

Dear Ms. Blank,

I am writing to apply for the Summer Internship position posted on MonsterTrak. I am a third-year student at the University of Chicago and am double-majoring in both Economics as well as English, with a minor in French. Employer Inc.'s focus solely on mergers and acquisitions appeals to my interest in learning more about this particular business segment.

My job last summer was an internship with Excellent Work Co. I learned how to effectively use different types of business intelligence software and present data from them in report form to my superiors. These very same skills will prove invaluable when analyzing possible buyers for the client and examining the details of impending integration.

Employer Inc.'s mergers and acquisitions focused, tight knit, and highly specialized business nature combined with my training background and motivation makes the Summer Intern position a perfect fit. My resume is also attached in this letter. I welcome an opportunity to discuss the position, details, and my qualifications further. I look forward to hearing from you and thank you for your consideration.

Sincerely,

Andrea Maroon

Analysis

Let's look at this paragraph-by-paragraph, using the simple rubric outlined above. The first paragraph is the "who and why" paragraph. How did Andrea do?

> *I am writing to apply for the Summer Internship position posted on MonsterTrak. I am a third-year student at the University of Chicago and am double-majoring in both Economics as well as English, with a minor in French. Employer Inc.'s focus solely on mergers and acquisitions appeals to my interest in learning more about this particular business segment.*

Not bad. She gets right to the point by explaining why she is applying for the job and where she heard about it. Next she introduces herself and her educational status.

Let's take a look at how she articulates her message. I think her wording of her specializations is a little awkward: "*Economics as well as English.*" Why would she want to de-emphasize her second major, English? A double major is a sign of high capacity and intellectual curiosity. The combination of English, Economics, and French is interesting, and gives me a sense of her well-roundedness. It should not be downplayed. I would rewrite this as follows:

> **I am writing to apply for the Summer Internship position posted on MonsterTrak. I am a third-year student at the University of Chicago double-majoring in Economics and English, with a minor in French.**

In fact, rearranging the sentences to emphasize her achievement reads a little better:

> **I am a third-year student at the University of Chicago double-majoring in Economics and English, with a minor in French. I am writing to apply for the Summer Internship position posted on MonsterTrak.**

Does she need to say any more? I already know in which pile to put her resume. What about this last sentence?

> *Employer Inc.'s focus solely on mergers and acquisitions appeals to my interest in learning more about this particular business segment.*

I would eliminate it. It breaks one of the cardinal rules of good cover letters: Ask not what the firm can do for you, but what you can do for the firm! In fact, it is worse than that because it reveals ignorance about mergers and acquisitions. Andrea hopes to learn about investment banking while she works for me. What if she does not like it? She will be a poor performer. I have ten other cover letters that say that mergers and acquisitions are the greatest things since sliced bread. Why would I take a risk on her? Would I nix her solely for this? Probably not; she is only a third-year student. However, if I have already seen a number of good resumes, I just might use this as an excuse to eliminate her. As a candidate, you never know. It is always best to avoid taking a risk if you can.

In the second paragraph, Andrea should be focusing on convincing me that she has the character and capacity to help me and my team succeed. Let's see how she does...

> *My job last summer was an internship with Excellent Work Co. I learned how to effectively use different types of business intelligence software and present data from them in report form to my superiors. These very same skills will prove invaluable when analyzing possible buyers for the client and examining the details of impending integration.*

Well, she has the right emphasis. She is providing me with information that she thinks will help my team, but there are a number of problems with the way she does it. Let's break this paragraph down sentence by sentence:

> *My job last summer was an internship with Excellent Work Co.*

There is nothing wrong with this sentence syntactically, but stylistically it is a waste of words. The exact same information could be relayed with a clause at the beginning of the following sentence:

> **Last summer at Excellent Work Co., I learned...**

The next sentence is good; it relays some real-world experiences that she learned:

> *I learned how to effectively use different types of business intelligence software and present data from them in report form to my superiors.*

Using software and presenting data are skills, not terribly selective skills, but that is okay. It is only a summer internship; I should not expect much more. Let's see if she digs any deeper into her passions or character and capacity in the last sentence.

These very same skills will prove invaluable when analyzing possible buyers for the client and examining the details of impending integration.

Nope, there is nothing more for me to build on. So far what I know is that she has intellectual curiosity from her double major and she has some general business experience, but this is probably not enough to persuade me to continue considering her for an interview slot.

Let's go back to this last sentence because there are a couple of major problems with its substance. First, the use of the words "will prove invaluable" is a strong statement of opinion, not fact. It is too strong to support her claim, which makes it an embellishment—a negative for her character. Second, she tries to sound like a savvy investment banker by using the phrase "impending integration," but it sounds more like a phrase contrived from a thesaurus. This sentence is a perfect example of a violation of risk minimization. She is telling me what the important skills are to run my business. Mind you, I did not ask her to state her opinion, but she did and she was wrong. Using business analysis software and presenting data are not "invaluable" skills to make my team successful. She has just killed her chances for further consideration.

Don't worry, there is a lot more about Andrea to like, but she just does not understand how and what to present to a prospective employer. Let's continue to the last paragraph and point out one more major problem, and then we will try to put this all back together with a little polish.

Employer Inc.'s mergers and acquisitions focused, tight knit, and highly specialized business nature combined with my training background and motivation makes the Summer Intern position a perfect fit. My resume is also attached in this letter. I welcome an opportunity to discuss the position, details, and my qualifications further. I look forward to hearing from you and thank you for your consideration.

Do you see the big problem? I'll give you a hint: It centers on the word "perfect." The first sentence of this paragraph is again quite an embellishment:

Employer Inc.'s mergers and acquisitions focused, tight knit, and highly specialized business nature combined with my training background and motivation makes the Summer Intern position a perfect fit.

There is nothing that she has said that would suggest that her skills are a "perfect fit" with Employer Inc. She just does not have a clear sense of what I am looking for her to say.

What can we do to help Andrea add some polish to this cover letter? Andrea is not that far off from making a much better presentation. One positive about her letter is that it is syntactically pretty well written and is very concise. Her main problem is that she does not know what her target audience is interested in hearing, nor does she understand what her key selling points are, nor how to effectively express them. What I know about Andrea from having seen her resume is that she is very active at school, she is in a number of clubs and intramural sports, and was even the co-founder of the women's lacrosse club. She played a key role in marketing the club and getting it to a critical number of participants.

What, if any, of this additional information would someone involved in investment banking, or any employer for that matter, find important? Well, we know that most employers value multi-tasking. Her double major and numerous activities suggest that this is a strength of hers. We also know that investment bankers are very competitive and often have to work under tight deadlines and extreme pressure. Perhaps examples from her participation in team sports could help here. Finally, her role in marketing the club shows potentially strong communication skills and salesmanship.

Armed with this simple analysis and a better understanding of Andrea's skill set, let's see if we can reconstruct a more polished cover letter that hits at more of her strengths. Before we do so we still need one more thing. Her analytical skills (using business software and presenting data) need more meat. To beef this up we are going to draw from a project she undertook during one of her economics classes. Finally, we are also going to add a new paragraph that focuses on her multi-tasking, team, and leadership skills. Okay, here we go:

I am a third-year student at the University of Chicago double-majoring in Economics and English, with a minor in French. I am writing to apply for the Summer Internship position posted on MonsterTrak.

Last summer at Excellent Work Co, I learned how to effectively use different types of business intelligence software and present data from them in report form to my superiors. Also, during my free time at school, I have used the analytical skills that I have learned in my classwork to analyze different stock trends and have developed a portfolio that I have begun to follow.

During my college career, I have made a point of becoming involved in many, varied extra-curricular activities. I very much enjoy the competitiveness and camaraderie of a team, and in addition to participating in a wide variety of intramural sports for my dorm, I am the co-founder of the first women's lacrosse club on campus. I am also actively participating in marketing the club within the university community and have taken the lead in organizing matches with other schools in the area.

I welcome an opportunity to discuss the position, details, and my qualifications further. I look forward to hearing from you and thank you for your consideration.

Sincerely,

Andrea Maroon

Perhaps not the best cover letter I have ever seen, but certainly much more appealing than Andrea's initial attempt.

Example 2: Andrew Nooram

Dear Recruiter:

I am in my penultimate year of undergraduate studies at the University of Chicago, and am working toward B.A.'s in Economics and Mathmatics. I have provided successful advice and analysis to my superiors in every role I have taken, which in turn has improved the measured efficiency of each organization I have been a part of. I want to bring this same success to the analyst position in your company.

My strengths lie in applying quantitative analysis to solving concrete problems. I am self-motivated and I enjoy shouldering additional responsibility for the group as a whole. As an intern at ABC Finance Advising last summer, I analyzed financial statements and wrote client communications with the securities analysis skills I picked up in Blue Chips last year. When I was finished with assigned work, I successfully modeled how a decrease in homeowners' equity brought about by falling real estate prices could affect the financial services demanded by various clients. I also calculated cross-variances amongst various investment instruments to maximize the amount of time the financial advisors spent with clients.

I enjoy working with a team to create new solutions to challenging problems. I am both a committee chair and one a sector leader within The Blue Chips, the leading financial services RSO on campus. As sector leader, I envisioned and implemented a mentoring system that has slashed the number of new members dropping out of the club to half the level encountered last year. To enhance our dominant position amongst other pre-professional clubs, I have organized events ranging from small gatherings with hedge fund managers to large presentations with upper management from leading investment banks as chair of the newly created Special Events Committee. I also co-founded our high school's Physics club, developing corporate sponsorships from Newco and Oldco into a volunteer internship/shadowing program for students from the club.

I believe I will bring much to your firm this coming summer. Thank you for reading my cover letter and resume, and I look forward to speaking with you soon.

Sincerely,

Andrew Nooram

Analysis

Once again, let's look at this paragraph-by-paragraph using the same rubric. The first paragraph is the "who and why" paragraph. How did Andrew do?

> *I am in my penultimate year of undergraduate studies at the University of Chicago, and am working toward B.A.'s in Economics and Mathmatics. I have provided successful advice and analysis to my superiors in every role I have taken, which in turn has improved the measured efficiency of each organization I have been a part of. I want to bring this same success to the analyst position in your company.*

Well, he started out okay. He told us a little bit about who he was, but then he gets a little off track. We will look at the relevance of the content in a minute, but first let's point out a couple of important facts he left out. First off, he does not mention the job to which he is applying. I don't know what pile to put his resume in! Second, I am not sure what degree he is getting. Is he majoring in both economics and mathematics or is he getting two degrees, one in economics and the other in math? Both are interesting but getting two degrees is more so and a sign of higher capacity. If this is the case, he needs to make sure I understand this.

What about the content? There are quite a few problems. The first is the use of the word "penultimate." It is a great word and he uses it appropriately (it means the next to last, by the way), but it is awkward. Some people might not know what it means—too risky. Next, did you find the typo? Andrew misspelled his own major! It's math"e"matics; oops!

What about the content of the second sentence?

> *I have provided successful advice and analysis to my superiors in every role I have taken, which in turn has improved the measured efficiency of each organization I have been a part of.*

First off, this information does not belong in the first paragraph of his letter. It does not help me determine what pile to put his resume in. Second, the statement "providing successful advice and analysis" is an opinion, not a fact, and thus is not salient. Third, what does "measured efficiency" mean? This is the type of language you want to avoid. You need to make it easy for your reader to understand your message. Andrew sounds like a statistics professor, not an analyst on my team.

What about the last sentence:

> *I want to bring this same success to the analyst position in your company.*

What is the "success" he is referring to? The measured efficiency? It is not clear. Andrew, like Andrea, does not understand what he should say to get my attention and obviously did not have someone else review his work.

Sorry, Andrew, but frankly I would have stopped after this first paragraph and put you in the NO pile. It is too bad; he really seems like he has talent, but I'll let some other employer take the risk on him.

Here is a possible rewrite:

> **I am a third-year student at the University of Chicago, and am working toward dual degrees in economics and mathematics. I recently attended an information seminar at the University of Chicago regarding summer employment opportunities at Your Company. I was especially interested in the quantitative analyst position about which your representative spoke and would like to be considered for one of the summer internship opportunities.**

Let's take a look at the next two paragraphs now. Andrew's goal in this part of the letter should be to highlight his general job skills and show evidence of his character and capacity. He has chosen to break this up into two paragraphs. The first one focuses on his job-related experience and the second on his team and leadership skills. Indications of his capacity are sprinkled throughout both.

Let's first look at his experiences. Remember, he should focus his arguments on what he is going to do for me and my team, not what he hopes I will do for him. How does he do?

> *My strengths lie in applying quantitative analysis to solving concrete problems. I am self-motivated and I enjoy shouldering additional responsibility for the group as a whole. As an intern at ABC Finance Advising last summer, I analyzed financial statements and wrote client communications with the securities analysis skills I picked up in Blue Chips last year. When I was finished with assigned work, I successfully modeled how a decrease in homeowners' equity brought about by falling real estate prices could affect the financial services demanded by various clients. I also calculated cross-variances amongst various investment instruments to maximize the amount of time the financial advisors spent with clients.*

Not too bad. He starts out with a good sentence talking about his strengths (and touches on a passion, too). Then, he shifts gears to character traits: self-motivation and willingness to work hard. Then, he gives an example of tangible experience applying this strength in analysis. Last, he gives me two examples of his self-motivation. This is all good stuff. What I get from this paragraph is that he is hard working, can work on his own, and has had a summer of relevant job experience. However, as the analysis below shows, he needs a fair bit of polish.

Let's look at the context and syntax sentence by sentence:

My strengths lie in applying quantitative analysis to solving concrete problems.

This is a pretty good start. I have a good idea of what kind of worker he is from this statement. Why? "Applying quantitative analysis to solve concrete problems" is not just a strength, it is probably close to one of his passions. The one problem I have with this statement is the use of the word "concrete." It has a couple of possible interpretations and, thus, could be a source of risk. I think what he is getting at is that Andrew likes solving non-abstract, real problems. He is making a distinction between real world, empirical problems and classroom, theoretical ones.

I have come to this realization after consulting the dictionary and spending upwards of 15 minutes thinking about this word in relationship to the context of his message in the whole cover letter. However, in the instance that someone is scanning Andrew's cover letter to see if he may be of interest to add to a team, "concrete" could be interpreted to mean a problem that has already been defined and preprocessed (such as his work reviewing financial statements). This would reveal him to be a limited-capacity employee.

This is why is it extremely important to have someone who knows nothing about the particular qualification of a particular job proofread your cover letters. She will flag these sorts of issues, not necessarily in the level of detail that I have, but enough to recognize the wording is a little awkward and enough to make you refine your thoughts a little more. For Andrew, I would make this clearer by replacing "concrete" with "real-world."

My strengths lie in applying quantitative analysis to solving real-world problems.

How about the next statement:

I am self-motivated and I enjoy shouldering additional responsibility for the group as a whole.

Again, this is another good statement. He has given me a couple of character traits that I should find appealing for someone on my team; he is a self-starter that enjoys working hard. The ending prepositional phrases ("for the group as a whole") are irrelevant and should be dropped.

So far Andrew has set this up pretty well; he has told me that he has good quantitative problem solving skills and is a self-motivated, hard worker. The rest of the paragraph should be filled with evidence to support these two statements.

Let's see how he did…

As an intern at ABC Finance Advising last summer, I analyzed financial statements and wrote client communications with the securities analysis skills I picked up in Blue Chips last year.

This is okay. It highlights a skill he has picked up that I will not have to train him to do, but it does not indicate that this is a "strength" or that he employed any quantitative skill to solve any real problems. The last part of this statement ("with the securities analysis skills I picked up in Blue Chips last year") is irrelevant and unclear and should be dropped.

The next sentence is good support of both his themes:

When I was finished with assigned work, I successfully modeled how a decrease in homeowners' equity brought about by falling real estate prices could affect the financial services demanded by various clients.

He is self-motivated because he did this after his "assigned work" and he shows aptitude for problem solving. If he had used quantitative techniques in the modeling it would have been more powerful to say so. This statement is a little too specific, but it works in this context because it adds nice support to the premise of the paragraph and it makes a nice hook for an interview question.

The last statement,

I also calculated cross-variances amongst various investment instruments to maximize the amount of time the financial advisors spent with clients.

demonstrates a possible problem-solving skill, but combined with the previous statement it makes the paragraph a little wordy and too detailed. I would make the following suggestions:

On my own initiative, I employed x and y quantitative techniques and successfully analyzed the impact of falling real estate prices on the financial services demanded by various ABC clients. I also developed a successful model using cross-variances to help maximize the financial advisor / client relationship.

Putting it all together, we have:

My strengths lie in applying quantitative analysis to solving real-world problems. I am self-motivated and I enjoy shouldering additional responsibility. As an intern at ABC Finance Advising last summer, I analyzed financial statements and wrote client communications. On my own initiative, I employed x and y quantitative techniques and successfully analyzed the impact of falling real estate prices on the financial services demanded by various ABC clients. I also developed a successful model using cross-variances to help maximize the financial advisor / client relationship.

In the next paragraph Andrew focuses on leadership and team skills:

I enjoy working with a team to create new solutions to challenging problems. I am both a committee chair and one a sector leader within The Blue Chips, the leading financial services RSO on campus. As sector leader, I envisioned and implemented a mentoring system that has slashed the number of new members dropping out of the club to half the level encountered last year. To enhance our dominant position amongst other pre-professional clubs, I have organized events ranging from small gatherings with hedge fund managers to large presentations with upper management from leading investment banks as chair of the newly created Special Events Committee. I also co-founded our high school's Physics club, developing corporate sponsorships from Newco and Oldco into a volunteer internship/shadowing program for students from the club.

44

Like the previous paragraph the content is good, but it is disorganized, too wordy and needs a lot of polish. Let's dig in.

To begin with, the content in this paragraph does not directly support the introductory sentence—what are the challenging problems for which he created new solutions? Instead of changing the body to fit the theme, it is probably better to change the theme to fit the body. I would try something like this:

I enjoy working in a team environment and taking on leadership roles.

Do I care that he "enjoy(s)" working in teams? Doesn't it go against the credo of "Ask not what the firm can do for you, but what you can do for the firm?" Maybe a little, but people often excel at things they enjoy doing, so in this case I think it is a positive.

In the next sentence, there are a couple of stylistic issues and a big "don't"—another grammatical mistake!

> *I am both a committee chair and one a sector leader within The Blue Chips, the leading financial services RSO on campus.*

Stylistically, "both" doesn't add anything and is just an extra word. Also, he uses an acronym, RSO. Anybody? Really Smart Outfit? Radical Socialist Organization? It is best to spell these acronyms out and not to assume a detailed level of knowledge on the part of the reader. Another sloppy mistake is "one a sector leader." I cannot stress this enough. Your cover letter has to be grammatically perfect. Every time that you make a change have someone proofread it. Have two people proofread it if you have the same problem that Andrew has.

Why are we incapable of effectively proofreading our own work? Because we read our own work the way we intended it to be written, not the way it actually is written. Andrew is not alone. Many people, including me, experience this same mental block. The lesson is: Don't trust yourself. It is too risky.

I would make the following changes to Andrew's sentence:

I am a committee chair and a sector leader of The Blue Chips, the leading financial services student organization on campus.

The next sentence is a bit of an embellishment:

As sector leader, I envisioned and implemented a mentoring system that has slashed the number of new members dropping out of the club to half the level encountered last year.

He "envisioned" a mentoring system? Perhaps "designed" would be a better word choice. He also claims to have "slashed" the number of dropouts. Again, this is a bit of an embellishment. It is a single-year variation and not worthy of such a strong statement.

Is this information even relevant? Yes, I think so. We will talk about "hooks" in more detail when we get to the resume section. This is an excellent lead-in for an interview question: How did he diminish the number of dropouts? We can make this a lot less risky by toning down the word choice and by making a subtle but positive inflection. Instead of "slashing" the drop-out rate, isn't it better to have "increased the retention level"?

As sector leader, I designed and implemented a mentoring system that has increased the retention level of new members by a third.

Let's look at the next sentence. There is a subtle but important problem with its context:

To enhance our dominant position amongst other pre-professional clubs, I have organized events ranging from small gatherings with hedge fund managers to large presentations with upper management from leading investment banks as chair of the newly created Special Events Committee.

I like the organization and leadership that it illustrates. This is good stuff, but why would he want to devalue this with the motivation "(t)o enhance our dominant position"? That is a silly reason to do these sorts of things. I think that he thinks that I think this kind of statement shows aggressiveness or competitiveness, but instead it shows a shallow character. It is much less risk to make this a "result" of his efforts instead of his motivation. See how much better the following reads:

As Chair of the Special Events Committee, I have organized events ranging from small gatherings with hedge fund managers to large presentations by upper management of leading investment banks. These events helped enhance The Blue Chips' dominant position amongst other financial services clubs.

Even so, I don't think the last statement adds too much and probably would err on the side of brevity and leave it out.

I hope that you appreciate the level of detail in this analysis of these examples. Learning from examples is really the best way to add polish to your cover letters. Studying the unifying theory on cover letters and resumes won't get you very far. You have to experience firsthand the mistakes and subtleties to master the art.

You may wonder how this level of detail is consistent with the premise that most prospective employers will not spend very much time reading your cover letter and probably won't see most of these subtle deficiencies.

I can speak from experience that many employers might not be able to articulate the subtle mistakes such as those Andrew and Andrea have made, but they will have seen other cover letters that do not have these problems. When they see words like "measured efficiencies," they will form a negative impression of you and that may be all that it takes to push your letter into the "no" category.

Finally, the last sentence:

> *I also co-founded our high school's Physics club, developing corporate sponsorships from Newco and Oldco into a volunteer internship/shadowing program for students from the club.*

There is only one small contextual mistake to make note of: Andrew's use of the word "our." It should be "his." But the bigger question is whether this information is relevant. It refers to his high-school days. I think Andrew has enough detail to support his topic sentence that this can be left off without losing much.

Let's put this back together and see how it reads:

> **I enjoy working in a team environment and taking on leadership roles. I am a committee chair and a sector leader of The Blue Chips, the leading financial services student organization on campus. As sector leader, I designed and implemented a mentoring system that has increased the retention level of new members by a third. As Chair of the Special Events Committee, I have organized events ranging from small gatherings with hedge fund managers to large presentations by upper management of leading investment banks. I also co-founded my high school's Physics club,**

developing corporate sponsorships from Newco and Oldco into a volunteer internship/shadowing program for students from the club.

I don't have too much to say about his closing paragraph:

I believe I will bring much to your firm this coming summer. Thank you for reading my cover letter and resume, and I look forward to speaking with you soon.

In general, I usually do not give them too much attention. Consider it a source of risk. There are more negative things that can come from it than positive. It is best to keep it short and sweet. Andrew's works in this regard.

So let's put this all together in 270 words versus the original 343:

Dear Recruiter,

I am a third-year student at the University of Chicago, and am working toward dual degrees in economics and mathematics. I recently attended an information seminar at the University of Chicago regarding summer employment opportunities at Your Company. I was especially interested in the quantitative analyst position about which your representative spoke and would like to be considered for one of the summer internship opportunities.

My strengths lie in applying quantitative analysis to solving real-world problems. I am self-motivated and I enjoy shouldering additional responsibility. As an intern at ABC Finance Advising last summer, I analyzed financial statements and wrote client communications. On my own initiative, I employed x and y quantitative techniques and successfully analyzed the impact of falling real estate prices on the financial services demanded by various ABC clients. I also developed a successful model using cross-variances to help maximize the financial advisor / client relationship.

I enjoy working in a team environment and taking on leadership roles. I am a committee chair and a sector leader of The Blue Chips, the leading financial services student organization on campus. As sector leader, I designed and implemented a mentoring system that has increased the retention level of new members by a third. As Chair of the Special Events Committee, I have organized events ranging from small gatherings with hedge fund managers to large presentations by upper management of leading investment banks.

I believe I will bring much to your firm this coming summer. Thank you for reading my cover letter and resume, and I look forward to speaking with you soon.

Sincerely,

Andrew Nooram

Conclusion

As one can see from the examples above, there is as much an art as there is a science to presenting information in a manner that will have the most impact. The art comes in through word choice and delivering your message in a manner that inspires the reader to hear it. The science comes in through the supporting evidence that you provide and your ability to deliver your message in a concise, unembellished, factual way.

Let's review the key insights to adding polish to your cover letter:

- Do utilize concise, factual statements that focus on what you can do for prospective employers, not what you expect to get from them.
- Do focus on your strengths and have examples that illustrate them.
- Don't delve into the details of your previous tasks. Do highlight your skills.
- Do individualize letters for each company.
- Do write a letter that is well-organized and easy to read:
  - Paragraph 1: Who you are and to what job you are applying.
  - Paragraph 2: Why you will make my team better:
    - Relevant experience and analytical skills
    - Relevant team, organizational, and leadership experiences and skills
  - Paragraph 3: Thank you. Short and sweet.
- Don't send out a letter that has not been proofread by at least one, preferably two, other people.

Examples of what not to say in your cover letter
(and my sarcastic comments!)

Though my long term goal is to work at a small firm, I feel the best way for me to gain experience is to work at a well established firm like XYZ Corporation.

> *Sure, I'm more than happy to train you so you can go work for someone else. Would you like to take some proprietary information with you as well?*

...my strong analytical skills and capacity to learn new skills quickly, which makes up for the fact that I have had little exposure to the retail industry so far.

> *Thanks for pointing out that weakness. Any other reasons you shouldn't get the job that you want to point out?*

Overall, with my significant business background, I feel that I am a perfect fit for XYZ Corporation.

> *And only a sophomore in college. Amazing that you not only gained all the experience at such a young age, but also understand how it fits "perfectly" with my company. Must be a savant; there can be no other explanation.*

With a deep and keen willingness to learn I am applying for the Business Analyst position...

> *I am not sure what "deep" and "keen" have to do with anything; however, I am not hiring you to learn but to do. Perhaps if you had "deep" and "keen" understanding of my business that would be relevant.*

I was thrilled to find the internship suits my aspirations and interests enabling me to wholeheartedly serve and enrich your company.

> *Must have collaborated with the guy above. You might be thrilled, but I am underwhelmed. Don't waste my time.*

I have gained a strong mathematical ability by planning bingo.

> *What about your command of 5/26ths of the English alphabet (B-I-N-G-O)? You might want to include that too.*

I feel that XYZ Corporation would offer me the opportunity to work in a challenging and stimulating environment while fostering me potential for growth.

Probably would not have read far enough to see the typo!

I am writing concerning the opening you have for a business analyst. I would like to request an interview for this position, as I am a perfect fit both for this position and your company. An interview would be mutually beneficial for both XYZ Corp. and myself.

Another savant. How do they know this stuff with such certainty?

I have developed outstanding communication skills, in the way that I was directly responsible for maintaining relations with over forty City-based nonprofit organizations.

Huh? How can you throw me "outstanding communication skills" with a sentence that makes no sense?

In *The Wealth of Nations*, Adam Smith argues that humans, compared to all other beings, constitute a social society because we exchange. The financial services industry with its many unique opportunities and challenges is at the core of the interchange of commodities and securities and thus, as Smith would agree, the force that both preserves and advances society. This commanding role is what attracts me most to the financial services industry. My name is …

Ugh, 95 words of blabber before he gives me his name. Adam Smith is as dead as your chance of getting an interview.

…your company's energetic work environment and commitment to the professional and leadership development of its employees, through a comprehensive training program and one-on-one mentorship, have convinced me that a career at XYZ is an ideal one.

Not only do I not care, but you're a brown-noser!

I am convinced that this internship can provide me with a unique learning experience for me to enhance my skills and to explore my interest in business.

No thanks, I'll take the guy that tells me about the skills that he will provide that will make my team better.

The position of a Business Analyst will provide me the tools and knowledge on how to become a professional analyst that I can apply in various industries.

> *Great! Just what I wanted to hear. You are going to use me and then apply your skills elsewhere.*

..[I'll] be a great asset to your company in its effort to become the best.

> *To "become" the best. Ouch! I thought we were the best.*

My analytical and communication skills make me a perfect candidate for a job at your company and my interest in business and willingness to increase my knowledge in the filed will help me quickly settle into the position.

> *Hmm, a rambling, impersonal statement with a typo and a grammatical error is a perfect example of communication skills I am looking for.*

The second that I saw your advertisement for the position, I knew that your company would provide an exceptional place for me to put my communication and organizational skills to the test. That your company provides a high-stakes, strongly established arena for testing those skills is a draw that I could not ignore.

> *Wow, the second you saw the ad you were able to absorb that much detail about my firm. Huh, then why does this sound so much like a canned statement that you put on all your cover letters? Either way, it is wasted words. I only learned what you want, not what you will give.*

My exemplary customer service skills and impeccable work ethic would lend themselves perfectly to the position of Business Analyst at XYZ Corporation.

> *Wow, three superlatives in one sentence! You would expect his letter to be teeming with supporting facts, wouldn't you? Well, he did mention that he worked as a Sales Associate at a clothing retailer for the summer, but that did not quite do it for me.*

My expansive expertise would allow me to excel in the Business Analyst position currently offered.

> *Dictionary.com had a few definitions of "expansive":*
>> 1. *Having a wide range or extent; comprehensive; extensive*
>>
>> *...*
>>
>> 6. *Psychiatry. Marked by an abnormal euphoric state and by delusions of grandeur*
>
> *Which one do you think is more appropriate?*

I am excited about the opportunity to gain valuable experience in the merchandising industry. As the son of an owner of a marketing consulting agency, I have always had a passion for business…

> *Perhaps if you mentioned that your mother loved to shop, there might be some correlation.*

I am very excited about the opportunity to work at Morgan Stanley…

> *Good for you! It is a great firm, but, being that I work for a rival institution, it may make more sense to let them know directly.*

I have gained a strong understanding of the criminal justice system from my son who is a convicted meth dealer.

> *Uh, no comment.*

V.   Resumes

As with cover letters, there is not one definitive structure to a well-designed resume, but in this chapter we will discuss some very important strategic layout issues and outline some of the most common pitfalls.

Precious Real Estate

The one axiom of a polished resume is that location matters. When you are designing your resume, you should place your most important attribute, the one that sells you the most, at the top of your resume. Think of the layout of your resume as similar to that of a newspaper. The top of your resume is your "headline." It is what people see first. It is what tempts them to make a "purchase"—an investment of their time—and continue reading.

For most college and graduate students, their "headline" is their current education. For someone with relevant work experience, it will most likely be your most recent job. The farther one goes down the page, the less valuable the real estate, and the less likely something near the bottom of your resume will catch a recruiter's eye.

Layout

I have seen many different styles and themes for a resume, and there is some leeway that one can employ to fit his or her personality, but be careful. From just the layout of your resume, without reading any of the content, I can learn a lot about you. I can ascertain your attention to detail, your organizational skills, your level of maturity, your judgment, your ego, and your ability to work well with others. Basically, it tells me a lot about what kind of person you are and can shape my initial impression of you before I even get to the details.

Initial impressions are key. Remember that in the initial steps of the resume review process, I am first and foremost trying to weed people out. Perhaps it will be subconscious, but the layout of your resume will create the first impression. Before the first word is read, a good layout will project a positive feeling and may start an applicant out in the "yes" pile. A bad layout can have the opposite effect. Like it or not, it is human nature to look for evidence to confirm initial feelings so with a poor layout, you will be starting with a handicap from which you might not be able to recover.

Key Points

The most salient elements of a resume resemble those of a cover letter, with a few key nuances:

Avoid typos and grammatical errors. There is even less tolerance for sloppiness in a resume than in a cover letter. Perhaps a recruiter will overlook a grammatical mistake on a cover letter, since these are produced quickly and must be adapted often, but not on your resume. It should be thoroughly reviewed many times by many different eyes and should be perfect.

Be concise. Many people make the mistake of listing everything that they have done. It is important not to leave any large chronological holes on your resume, but too much detail can dilute the main message. A good rule of thumb is to limit the number of supporting bullet points under current and recent entries to no more than three. Use even fewer bullets for listings of earlier experience.

Also, keep support bullets general. Specific details will rarely help you at this point, and notwithstanding the issues of added risk and dilution of your main message, the reviewer may not be able to translate the relevance of the specific tasks.

Use 11-point font or larger. Please don't play games with your font size. If you have a new, relevant experience or educational achievement to add, by definition something else on your resume has just become less important and should be cut completely or collapsed. Don't try to squeeze everything in. If you do you will be setting the wrong first impression: "Wow, look at all these words. This person must think a lot about him or herself!" You have just entered into the "not likely" camp from where few return.

Slogging through a pile of resumes is never at the top of my daily agenda and it usually is performed near the end of the day on airplanes or on the commute home. By then, my eyes are tired and I am easily irritated. Having to squint to read your resume in 9-point font will not help your cause.

Make entries parallel. When organizing bullets under an experience heading, please follow the common grammatical law of parallelism. This means start ALL bullets with the same sentence structure, that is, action verbs or subjects. Here is a bad example to illustrate this point:

- *Only participant from the University of Chicago to be selected* ... (subject)
- *Worked most closely with* ... (past tense verb)
- *Responsible for giving* ... (present tense verb)

Bullets should be listed by relevance, with the most important first. 99.9% of the time this will be in chronological order, with the most recent first.

Avoid jargon and acronyms. Don't think that using acronyms and job-specific lingo makes you sound like you have experience or know what you are talking about. This only works if I understand them, too. You can probably get away with acronyms such as USA, S&P, or NFL, but most below this level of recognition are just a source of risk. Here is a bad example to illustrate this:

- *Helped compile a valuation deck with DCF, LBO, and Comparable Company Analyses*

Huh? All I really get from this statement is that he or she compiled something and it might have something to do with equity investment or investment banking.

Don't discuss proprietary information or divulge customer names. This shows poor judgment and a lack of ethical awareness. It is fatal.

- *Collaborated with Big Accounting Firm audit team to prepare SEC form 6-K for Joe's Media*

The only interviews that you will get are from people who want to see if they can get some information from you.

Don't embellish or state opinions. This is a source of risk. You have to be able to defend every word on your resume. Avoid superlatives like "excellence," "the best," "expert knowledge," "superior," or the like, unless you can strongly defend them.

Here is an interesting example from a resume that illustrates this point:

- *Exhaustively analyzed the state of the U.S. economy...*

This statement is a great "hook." It will spur many interview questions. However, the word "Exhaustively" completely changes the tenor of the question that I would ask and dramatically changes the risk/reward payoff of the hook. Let me explain what I mean by risk/reward payoff.

If the bullet point had merely stated "analyzed the state of the U.S. economy...," it would have been a useful hook and would have spurred me to ask which tools you used to analyze the U.S. economy. I may not like the substance of your answer, but it is opinion-free and fact-based. It has very little risk but has the possibility of a nice reward, that is, you could have mentioned knowledge of a couple of interesting tools that are relevant to the job for which I am hiring. This could lead to additional questions that hit a vein of relevant information that highlights your strengths and capacity.

However, by including the word "Exhaustively," you are stating an opinion about the level of your work. I am going to now ask you a completely different question and am going to have much higher expectations from your answer. I might directly ask you, "Why would you say that the analysis you did on the U.S. economy was exhaustive?" I will expect you to answer the question to meet my opinion of what exhaustive analysis is.

Chances are that I have a more advanced understanding of the subject than you and will be dissatisfied with your answer. However—here is where the concept of risk/reward payoff is interesting—if you are able to go head-to-head with me and meet my expectation of what exhaustive analysis is, you are likely to make a very strong impression. We will both have that tingly feeling: you because you just exposed one of your passions (and know that you nailed the question) and I because I found someone with strong character and a high capacity.

The moral of the story is that you need to back up and be able to defend every word on your resume. If you cannot, than it should not be on there.

Populate your resume with general statements that illustrate:

- Good judgment
- Competitiveness
- Excellence and high level of achievement
- Teamwork
- Passion
- Leadership
- Well-roundedness
- Taking the initiative
- Multi-tasking

The subject matter of these attributes is not important. The resume reviewer will be able to translate their usefulness to his or her work environment.

Hanna Hyde Gray

1234 W. University Blvd
Collegetown, MX
Hanna.gray@university.edu
312-555-5555

EDUCATION

The University of Collegetown Collegetown, MX

Bachelor of Arts in Economics Expected: June 20xx

- Cumulative GPA: 3.7/4.0
- Dean's List 20xx-20xx

Collegetown Careers in Business Studies

- Enrolled in a selective three year program focusing on business preparation and strategies
- Program includes graduate school of business coursework and extensive workshop training

National University Paris, France

Summer credit for French Language June 20xx-Sept. 20xx

EXPERIENCE

Mon Ami Learning Center Paris, France

Junior Academic Tutor, English Department June 20xx-Sept. 20xx

- Established English reading and writing program for students grades 4-6
- Prepared native-French, high school students in English grammar, essay-writing, and speech

Joe Statesman for Lt. Governor Campaign Hometown, MX

Finance Assistant, Finance Division June 20xx- Aug. 20xx

- Organized finances and donations of more than $1,000,000 using Access database
- Coordinated volunteer mailing events and compiled donor information lists using Microsoft Excel

LEADERSHIP / ACTIVITIES

Student Government College Council, University of Collegetown May 20xx – Present

- Initiated printing project to integrate and enhance printing services around campus
- Examine new funding models to improve allocation process to student organizations
- Approve committee chairs and Student Government Finance Committee's budget recommendations

Committee on Recognized Student Organizations, University of Collegetown Oct. 20xx – Present

- Drafted proposal to reform reapplication process for student organizations
- Approve potential student organizations and organization name changes
- Designate spaces for all event and storage requests

SKILLS

Fluent in conversational French and Spanish

John Harper Boyer

1234 South College Rd, Centerville, ST   john.boyer@state.edu – 201 -555-5555

EDUCATION

THE STATE UNIVERSITY   Centerville, State
Bachelor of Arts in Economics   Expected: June 20xx
- Cumulative GPA: 3.7/4.0 (Dean's List 20xx-20xx)

State University Program in Business
- Enrolled in a selective three year program focusing on business preparation and strategies.
- Program includes State Graduate School of Business coursework and extensive workshop training.

ACME INTERNATIONAL RESEARCH PROGRAM ABROAD   Capital, State
- Undertook primary research to enhance revenues of farmers in rural western State.   20xx-20xx
- Analyzed economic activity / underlying productivity within State Agro Sector.

WORK EXPERIENCE

CONGLOMERATE BANK   Capital, State
Summer Intern, Corporate Banking   June 20xx- August 20xx
- Created Trade Finance database using MS Excel for corporate client accounts.
- Designed and planned team-building projects and assisted to sell and monitor trade finance products.

CAPITAL BROADCASTING CORPORATION   Capital, State
Radio Jockey, Production Assistant, X-Chill FM   Summer 20xx
- Hosted as a Radio Jockey for a daily 4-hour talk show on a National Radio station.
- Integrated new subjects such as music, current city events and world issues into show and presented with local celebrities.

LEADERSHIP EXPERIENCE

South Assetia Students Association (SASA), The State University   Sept. 20xx to Present
Community Service Chairperson
- Arranging community projects with a social focus for SASA, specifically SHOUT, a street children non-governmental organization.
- Initiating and organizing a premier for a documentary film on SHOUT for a State filmmaker.

Global Enterprise Challenge, Capital   June 20xx
Managing Director
- Primary responsibility of devising product aimed at reducing global warming on a domestic level.
- Spearheaded the creation of a prototype, business plan, and presentation in a time-span of 24 hours.

School Yearbook, United College of Capital   20xx – 20xx
Editor-in-Chief
- Selected and lead a team of 70 students for all departments of production of 400-page yearbook.
- Collaborated with team members to conceptualize and develop themes, designs, layout, and content.
- Stimulated sales through increased marketing days and promotion efforts.

ACTIVITIES

Acme Consulting, Consultant   Centerville, State
- Contribute as a consultant on projects with University/ Centerville based clients.   20xx-Present
- Identify avenues for research, collecting primary data and conduct analysis for recommendations of business restructuring for current client.

SHOUT: Non Governmental Organization, Volunteer   Capital, State
- Contributed in teaching activities for SHOUT across Capital slum-areas and school sites.   20xx
- Currently work through correspondence to raise awareness and aid in fundraising.

SKILLS AND INTERESTS

- Language Skills – Fluent in Bangonese
- Computer Applications – Proficient in Macintosh and Windows operating systems and MS Office
- Sports – Golf, Badminton; Proficient in Modern/Chinese dance choreography

What is your first impression of the two resumes?

For me, the first is nicely spaced and pleasing to the eyes. I have a positive feeling from it and feel good about reading it. The second one is hard to quickly scan. Its different font sizes and poor spacing make it hard to find the relevant information.

I have just made a subjective decision about these two resumes without even looking at the content. I like the first one but do not like the second. The first one starts as a "Yes" and I will be looking to confirm this initial reaction as I scan the content of the resume; the second starts as a "No" and I will be looking to confirm this initial reaction as I scan the content of the resume. Sometimes I control this bias better than other times. I cannot even tell you that this bias is based on some factual basis. I think it is. I think that there is a correlation between the design of a resume and likelihood of success at getting a job, but I cannot say for certain. I can only tell you that when I see what I consider a poorly designed resume, it sets off alarm bells in my brain and influences the way that I will read and interpret the information on the page.

Outline of a Successful Resume

On average I spend about 30 seconds to a minute scanning your resume in search of relevant facts to support your cause. What are the key points that I am looking for? Each resume should have three main parts: educational history, relevant experiences, and interests and activities. Here is what I look for in each of the sections. These are the points that you want to make it easy for the reviewer to see:

Education

- Quality of school and major.
- GPA. For current students or newly matriculating students GPA is important.
- Something that is interesting about the candidate: foreign study, double major, multiple degrees, interesting research work.
- Evidence of a capacity for, and love of, learning.

Relevant Experience

- What are the skills that you have? How relevant are they to my team?
- Evidence of doing "real stuff" like research, analysis, marketing, and organization. Grunt work is "real stuff," too. I don't need the details, but it is good experience.
- Teamwork; experience working in a team environment.

Activities / Interests

- Evidence of competitiveness: Team sports or intellectual challenges demonstrate this.
- Ability to multi-task. Show me you are a busy person with a lot of balls in the air.
- A variety of interests: Are you well-rounded, with intellectual curiosity?
- Evidence of teamwork and leadership.

Overall

- Evidence of good judgment, multi-tasking, overachievement, willingness to work hard, and conscientious conduct.
- Examples that show an interest in my company's field.
- Ideology that fits with my company's culture.

It is important to note some of the things I am not looking for:

- Test scores. These are rarely relevant.
- High school information.
- Descriptive information about your past firms and organizations.
- Tasks that you performed.

Hooks

Before we drill down into the organization of your resume and look at some real-life examples, let me spend a little energy expounding on the concept of "hooks."

A hook is a statement or phrase in your resume or cover letter that is designed to pique interviewers' interest. It is a natural setup for an interview question that will illustrate a strength or evidence of your character or capacity. Good hooks are concise, general, easy-to-find examples of projects, skills, competitiveness, multi-tasking, initiative-taking, teamwork, awards, activities, interests, or travel.

Here are a few hooks to illustrate the point:

- Summer immersion program in Spanish language and culture.
- Organized and formed first campus stand-up comedy review.
- Wrote paper on the impact of globalization on sub-Saharan Africa.
- Analyzed and improved the organization of my club's travel schedule.
- Developed a database to capture changing trends in customer buying habits.
- Developed a program to advertise and market tiddlywinks club to new students.

The subject matter is not what is important. Many times people will not include something in their resume because they don't think the subject matter is relevant to the job. This is a mistake. It is the skills that are important.

Take the last example. "Tiddlywinks" is likely to be irrelevant in most every job search you do, but this statement is full of rich information that provides evidence of character and capacity. It shows initiative, leadership, passion, and well-roundedness as well as exposure to two skills: advertising and marketing, which may be important in many business situations.

Hooks are not just important for organizing your resume in a way that maximizes your advantages, but perhaps more important, hooks are helpful during an interview. Many times the second- or third-year associate who will determine your fate during your first-round interview is under-prepared. She might be filling in for someone who had a pressing deadline and is going into the interview cold. Most likely, she reviewed your cover letter and resume a couple of weeks ago and spent only a couple of minutes immediately before the interview refreshing herself with your background. You have to help her get up to speed quickly on your qualifications. Adding hooks makes this easy and allows her to focus on what you want her to. This will implicitly steer the interview in the most advantageous way.

If you design your resume with too many extraneous words, the interviewer might miss your most relevant attributes. Let's expand the tiddlywinks example a little further. Here is a typical section of a poorly "hooked" resume:

University Tiddlywinks Club

- Club promotes the game of tiddlywinks on campus and organizes tournaments for tiddlywinks enthusiasts. Currently there are 24 club members.
- Participated in 10 tournaments playing both doubles and singles. Voted best player 2008 and most improved player 2007. Won two singles titles and 2 doubles titles.
- As chairman of the membership committee, I promoted the club to new students holding two mixers and organizing a booth at the university club night.

The first bullet is a typical mistake that a lot of resume writers make. It provides descriptive information about the company or organization, not about the resume writer. It provides no relevant information that anyone outside the tiddlywinks "industry" would find important. The title conveys this in sufficient detail. The bullet point is hook-less.

The second bullet could perhaps hook the reader by implying competitiveness and dedication, but there is much more detail than is appropriate. We will explain why shortly. Most interviewers will think that it is trivial and won't bother to explore the relevance.

The third bullet has the best hook. Unfortunately, by the time the reviewer gets to this point, he has probably had enough with tiddlywinks and will not even read the one possibly interesting point in the section! There is too much detail in the third bullet, but it touches on some possible transferable skills. This is another common design flaw with many resumes. People tend to place the best things, the skills, buried in the last or next-to-last bullet. This is a big mistake. You need to get the relevant information out there first, not hide it in a sea of extra words.

Why? For one simple reason: People will be scanning your resume for relevant information and they are going to start with the first bullet. If they do not see what they want, they might not read any further!

Compare the following "hook-rich" description with the previous one:

University Tiddlywinks Club

- Developed a program to advertise and market the club to new students.
- Won four tournaments and voted best player in 2008.

I would argue that these two concise statements are much more powerful than the previous verbose bullets. There are so many different questions that even someone completely unprepared could conjure up:

- Tell me about the program you developed to promote the tiddlywinks club.
- What marketing and advertising strategies did you employ to attract new members?
- How successful were you?
- What does it take to be a champion in tiddlywinks?
- What was your highest-pressure situation during tournament play and how did you handle it?

The important point to remember when you are designing your resume is that you have to understand the context in which your information will be reviewed. You have to make it as easy as possible on your reader. Thinking about creating many hooks to "reel in" your interviewers is an effective, worthwhile exercise.

Objective Statement

By the way, I have not spoken about having an Objective at the top your resume. I do not have a strong opinion on the subject, except that you should only use it if you have a somewhat narrow focus of what you want to do. A bland general statement is worthless. "Seeking a career in the Financial Services" or "Healthcare Industry" is too broad. Best not to try to use your "Objective" statement to help answer this question.

Resume Sections in Detail

With the concept of hooks fresh in our minds, let's drill down on the specific sections of your resume: education, relevant experience, activities, and interests.

Education

For those of you who have two or more years of relevant job experience this section is rather rote: name of institution, degree, and major. You can add any prestigious awards or anything else that might differentiate you, but it's best to keep it short and sweet. The quality of the institution you attended may have some influence, but it is your relevant job experience that will matter the most. Feel free to skip to the next section.

For the rest of you who will be touting your education as a major selling point, here are some useful tips to give your education section some polish.

> **GPA:** This is probably one of the most important data points that recruiters will consider. Many Wall Street and consulting firms screen first on GPA. If yours is high, then you should definitely include it on your resume. If you leave it off, I will assume that it is low. However, if it is low, then you should leave it off; I am assuming that it is low, so leaving it off will not hurt you. For many jobs it may be only one of a number of criteria that is evaluated, so adding it only highlights a possible negative. What is considered low? It varies but generally a GPA below a 3.0 (B average) should be omitted.
>
> I have seen people who calculate their GPA out to four decimal places. This creates a negative impression on me. It shows poor judgment and too much attention to detail. It is impossible to differentiate potential career success between a 3.1 and 3.2 student or a 3.6 and 3.7 student, so representing yourself as a 3.667 student is trivial. Round up. I don't care. If you must get fancy, please make sure that the number of decimal places in the numerator matches the denominator. A 3.7/4.0 is beautiful. A 3.667/4.000 is overkill but consistent. A 3.667/4.0 is sloppy. If you are exactly a 3.25 or a 3.75, it is ok to represent this out to two decimal points.

Relevant coursework: If you don't have much work experience and you need to add relevant hooks, this is a good place to do so, but please make sure that the courses are relevant and you excelled at them. Remember that you must be able to defend everything on your resume. Make sure you can answer these three questions about each course mentioned:

1. Why do you think this course is relevant to this job opportunity?
2. How well did you do in this course?
3. What was the most interesting thing you learned or problem you solved in this course?

Previous educational information: The half-life of relevant past educational experiences is short. This is especially true with high school information. Remember your resume is precious real estate. If you chose to place your educational information on the top of your resume, it is especially important to avoid wasting space with irrelevant, outdated information. Here is a great example of wasting precious real estate. This is from an international University of Chicago student:

....

Education

University of Chicago   Chicago, Illinois
Bachelor of Arts in Economics   June 20xx
  • Cumulative GPA: 3.5/4.0

Capital High School   Capitalcity, Foreignland
  • GPA 5.0/5.0
  • Received full financial aid at the only high school in Foreignland for gifted and talented students.
  • Honors: Highest Honors (awarded to students with GPA above 4.25/5.00), Academic Achievement Awards for Foreign Language and Music Departments, Honor Board's Award.

....

Look how much space he spends on his high school relative to his college.

Why is this a mistake? The high school information sounds impressive, but most people will not have specific enough knowledge to know the relevance of any of these data. If he is trying to make the impression that he is smart, it isn't necessary; I already have a measure of that from the university GPA. This is a relative measure that I understand. This other information only dilutes the message and introduces risk. What are the risks? Poor judgment that he thinks that this is important, for one.

Bottom line: There is a natural tendency for young people to think it is important to put down everything remotely important on their resumes. A corollary of this is that they hesitate to take something off their resumes once it becomes outdated. Fight these urges.

When might such information be relevant? Rarely, but there is one case where dated educational information (or any information for that matter) might make sense: when you are trying to make a specific connection. For instance, if the international student above was applying to a company that had a disproportionate number of Capital High School graduates in its ranks, he might hit upon someone who understands and appreciates this information. Likewise, if you are applying to a job posting in your hometown, especially if your university experience may not be too familiar there, you may want to drop a name that will make you more familiar.

This kind of connection can be very powerful in certain situations. But my recommendation is that it is better to fish for a connection in the interests/activities section (or cover letter) where the real estate is less expensive.

Entrance exam test scores: SAT and ACT scores should only be used if your GPA does not fully translate your intellectual capacity. This may be the case if you are attending a school that does not have a national reputation or your GPA is below average. Otherwise, at best, your test scores will be redundant and may be a source of risk. Why is her GPA so low when she scored so well on the SAT? Leave them off. You may be proud of them, but I probably don't care.

Why don't I care? Two reasons: first, it is most likely dated material. You take the SAT and ACT in the junior or senior year of high school. You know how I feel about high school information. Second, a proclivity to perform well on multiple choice tests is not a skill that translates well into most job settings.

Awards: The big question with an award: Is it relevant? Does it say something about your character or capacity? If you are a Phi Beta Kappa or Fulbright Scholar, this is a brand that people will know. Lesser awards may not be as recognizable but could still be valuable hooks. If the award will help an interviewer glean something favorable about your character or capacity, then it might make sense to include it. The question of relevance is not whether it is directly related to the job, but whether it exposes a character trait that may be.

Through high school, I had a morning paper route and won a college scholarship from my local paper. This scholarship was partly based on academic achievement and partly based on long-term service. It is the latter that makes it worth including. It illustrates a certain level of persistence and dedication. These are traits that many employers like to see.

International study: I am a big fan of international exposure. Any time that someone goes outside her comfort zone, she increases her character and capacity and learns a lot about herself. She is closer to the Oracle. Without hesitation add this to your resume.

Education Hooks

The education section of your resume should be brief and factual, but there is still an opportunity to give a strong impression of your character and capacity. Here are some things that I look for that are good sources of hooks:

> **Interest in my industry:** Let's start with the basics. Someone straight out of school might be smart and hit all the right buttons in her application, but might end up being a bad fit for an industry or specialization. Recruiters' defense against this unfavorable outcome is to look for people who have illustrated a genuine interest in the field in question. Perhaps a candidate is applying for a job in finance and took a business class as part of her liberal arts education, or is applying for a hospital administration position and wrote a paper on the healthcare crisis. When I review a resume, one question always comes first to my mind: Is there evidence that this person is interested in doing what I would be hiring her to do?

A well-placed entry about a relevant course or research thesis could help set the right tone for your resume.

Risk taking / continual learning: You can set up this hook by showing you have created a unique academic experience. Economics and business majors are a dime a dozen and listing these majors alone does not show much intellectual depth or well-roundedness. Couple one of these degrees with a study abroad program and a minor in theater, psychology, or statistics and I start to get a better picture of you.

I will talk more about this in the interview section, but I am very leery of students with near-perfect GPAs for fear that they are not risk takers. You know these people: those whose focus is solely on getting good grades, not learning for its own sake. I don't want these people working for me. If you have a near-perfect GPA, you need to show me something else so you don't get typecast incorrectly.

Practical problem solving skills: Schooling teaches the theory of things and develops interesting models. Business is about solving real-world problems. Evidence that you have solved real-world problems through research and analysis would be a useful hook.

Relevant Experience

For most people, this section is the meat of their resume and where they can highlight the relevant things they have done that will attract potential employers. For most seasoned workers, this section will consist of their most recent work experience listed in reverse chronological order: most recent to distant.

I will go into more detail as to how to add polish to this information, but first a word to those of you who are fresh to the working world and do not have much relevant work experience: This is a real weakness to your resume. You might be able to dazzle prospective employers with your brilliance during an interview, but you first have to get through the front door. As a potential boss, I need to see evidence from you that you are interested in my profession and that you have some practical business skills and can analyze and solve complicated problems.

Where might you get some of these skills? Well, chances are you already have them from your academic experience. Have you ever done a research project or team project? If the answer is yes, then try to fashion one of these into a relevant experience. The subject matter is not important. It is the skills and thought process that are important.

I had a candidate who was hesitant to mention that she worked in a lab for a biology professor because the subject matter was not relevant to finance. She missed the point that the hands-on, problem-solving skills she had learned in the lab are great assets in finance.

Haven't done anything like this yet? Well, it is very important and pretty easy to do. If you are still in school, tell one of your professors that you are interested in doing some research. Chances are he will see this as an opportunity to get some cheap labor and will set you off in the right direction. Whether you are in school or have graduated, get a part-time job or do volunteer work. Not willing to put out the extra effort? Don't expect me to want you on my team.

What makes the experience section of your resume stand out? By now you can probably predict what I am going to say. Yes, that is right: Keep it concise and general with plenty of hooks that highlight your strengths and passions. Here are key ideas to keep in mind:

- **Use no more than three supporting bullet points:** As a general rule, three bullet points are enough to explain most previous experiences. The shorter the duration and the more distant the experience, the less you want to say. It is a common practice when people update their resumes to slap on a new experience without editing their previous ones. Unless you are looking to shift gears back to what you previously were doing, you should liberally prune the information regarding your previous work experiences.

- **Maintain parallel structure:** Your bullet points should flow and should all start with action verbs or subjects (the former is much easier).

- **Include relevant and skill-based information:** For junior and mid-level positions, you should highlight what skills you used more than what you actually did.

Let's take a look at a few examples in need of polish that illustrate these points.

Example 1

The first is from a University of Chicago student with a 3.7 GPA:

....

Acme Investment Bank –Debt Capital Markets (DCM)   Summer 20xx

- *Only participant from the University of Chicago to be selected for this internship opportunity specific to college sophomores*
- *Worked most closely with Power Group and Hybrids Group within DCM*
- *Responsible for giving indicative pricings for new corporate bond issuances, creating weekly market updates for several sector groups in DCM and sending them to clients and other groups within Acme, creating pitchbooks, putting together working group lists for deals*
- *Assumed full-time analyst responsibilities in several pitches and witnessed the execution of several bond deals*
- *Gained proficiency in using Excel, PitchPro and Bloomberg*

By now a few problems should pop out right away. The first is the length. There is way too much irrelevant information. Remember your message should be tailored to the hirer.

In this context, let's take a look at each bullet. Is the first bullet relevant?

- *Only participant from the University of Chicago to be selected for this internship opportunity specific to college sophomores*

It is the first bullet, so it should be the most important. Does it help me determine if this person has the character and capacity or relevant skills to help my team grow? It does none of these things. In fact, it comes across as snooty. "I" was the only one chosen. So what?!

The second bullet is less offensive, but is equally irrelevant.

- *Worked most closely with Power Group and Hybrids Group within DCM*

A recruiter won't know what a "Power" or "Hybrid" group is, and won't care.

The third bullet is a perfect example of a task- versus skill-based message. Can you identify the tasks and the skills?

- *Responsible for giving indicative pricings for new corporate bond issuances, creating weekly market updates for several sector groups in DCM and sending them to clients and other groups within Acme, creating pitchbooks, putting together working group lists for deals*

The tasks are "giving indicative pricing," "creating and sending weekly market updates," "creating pitchbooks," and "putting together working group lists." Recruiters must infer skills learned from the tasks listed. There was some kind of communication involved and some organizational and analytical work, but it is unclear exactly what. If she is applying for a very narrow range of jobs only in Debt Capital Markets, then this level of detail may be appropriate and understandable to the resume reviewer, but for any position without this specific knowledge, tasks do not meaningfully transfer and the skills can only be vaguely inferred.

The fourth bullet has two parts. The first part, like the first bullet, is neither a task nor skill:

- *Assumed full-time analyst responsibilities in several pitches…*

It is meant to portray some sense of achievement, but "assumed" is a very weak action verb. Here is the problem with having something like this on your resume. Someone is going to ask you a question in an interview that goes something like this:

> ME: *"Tell me the circumstances that lead to your assuming full-time analyst responsibilities?"*
>
> YOU: *"Well, I was doing a great job and I was promoted."*
> Or
> YOU: *"Well, the analyst on the team left and I took over his responsibilities."*

The first response shows capacity and strong character, but if this is the likely response, don't you think she would have used a *stronger* action verb, such as "promoted," to convey this?

The second response shows only circumstance and does not infer any character traits. It fits the weak action verb "assumed."

When I am reading her resume I am going to assume that it is the second situation and take the weak verb for what it is worth. Thus, the whole point becomes unimportant.

The second part of this bullet has a passive verb "witnessed":

> *... and witnessed the execution of several bond deals*

I like the fact that she is honest and is not trying to make this experience sound more important than it was, but this passive verb does not convey a skill. I have witnessed Derrek Lee hit a 95-mph fastball into the bleachers at Wrigley field. This does not make me any more capable of replicating his achievement.

Finally, the fifth bullet is the first one that conveys any real skills:

> • *Gained proficiency in using Excel, PitchPro and Bloomberg*

Yes, these are skills. One might think that they are basic skills and are not very important. Perhaps they are not for a seasoned professional, but for a young professional looking for that first full-time position, one of these may be one of the five or so things that I am looking for in my new analysts.

Before we bring all these ideas together into a better description for this young lady, there is one syntactical problem with her bullets as well: parallelism. The first bullet starts with a subject phrase ("Only participant"); the second, fourth and fifth with past tense verbs ("Worked," "Assumed," "Gained"), and the third with a present tense verb ("Responsible"). This is very sloppy. One can learn a lot about a person just from how he or she organizes his or her resume. Sloppy resumes suggest sloppy workers.

Here is a more polished version:

....

Acme Investment Bank – Debt Capital Markets (DCM)   **Summer 20xx**

- **Communicated indicative pricings of new corporate bond issuances to customers**
- **Created weekly market updates for several sector groups**
- **Designed pitchbooks and gained proficiency in Excel, PitchPro, and Bloomberg**

31 words versus 96 words without, in my view, any loss in content. Brilliant!

Notice how I made this much more compact and skill-centric. Remember, what I am looking for are the skills that she learned and that she had some exposure to something relevant. In a summer internship, I am not expecting much more. So don't bore me with the details.

If this had not been her most recent work experience, I would even consider shortening it further:

....

Acme Investment Bank – Debt Capital Markets (DCM)   **Summer 20xx**

- **Created weekly market updates and designed pitchbooks**
- **Gained proficiency in Excel, PitchPro and Bloomberg**

Example 2

Let's look at a second example from a University of Chicago student with a GPA of 3.75 describing his summer internship at a large investment bank:

- *Created test worksheets in Excel to document whether IBD policies and procedures are being followed and whether adequate risk controls in the Big City Investment Banking offices are in place*
- *Assisted in the scoping and testing phases of a thematic review of Travel and Entertainment expense reporting for all Big City Private Wealth Management sales desks*
- *Interviewed over 25 Private Wealth Advisors to gain an understanding of the controls surrounding travel and entertainment expense reporting*
- *Worked in a team of 12 interns to create a department-specific Wiki page, a Policies and Procedures site, and a database of employees skills: three business tools which will facilitate the department's operations and increase efficiency*

This is a very interesting example because he does a good job listing the skills he performed, but they are intermixed with tasks and irrelevant information. There are way too many uninteresting details that dilute his message.

 I will save you the analysis and give you the polished version:

- **Performed test work to determine whether policies and procedures are being followed in the Big City Investment Banking offices**
- **Communicated with over 25 Private Wealth Advisors to evaluate the controls surrounding expense reporting**
- **Collaborated with four interns to create a department-specific information portal, a Policies and Procedures Web site, and a database of employee skills**

57 words versus 114 words. It is still boring but is much easier to read and has a number of useful hooks. By the way, it was the student himself who made these improvements, which proves that with a little direction you can add polish to your resume as well!

Activities (Soft Skills)

So far we have covered the two most important areas of your resume, and for the most part there is not a lot of value, only risk, in deviating from the standard script. However, as we venture down the page, and the real estate gets a little cheaper, there is more room for customization and self-expression. The standard rubric for the rest of the page is a section on activities and then a short section on interests. However, some resumes successfully replace the activities section with "Leadership," "Teamwork," "Volunteering," or "Research." All of these departures are fine as long as the objective of doing so is to highlight the uniqueness of your strengths and spotlight your character and capacity.

I am looking to hire well-rounded, interesting people. Well-rounded people with multiple interests and talents are adaptable and will be able to grow as my business grows. A strong activities section will give me insight about a candidate's future potential.

Here are some key insights to help you hone your message:

- **Put stuff down:** I want to see that you are well-rounded and can multi-task. Don't think that just because something you did is not directly related to your expectation of tasks you will be performing in your new career that it is not relevant. I was once interviewing a candidate for a position that required focus under pressure and a high degree of attention to detail. What got this fellow the job was not his education or his past experiences. These were important contributing factors, but what won me over was that he was an expert marksman. After quizzing him about this hobby, I learned that marksmanship is a repetitive function and to be an expert requires great focus, concentration and attention to detail. That was exactly what I needed! He had developed a skill that was likely to translate into my work environment. And it did.

- **Competitiveness:** Being competitive is a good thing and should be stressed. In one of my workshops at the University of Chicago, I was amazed that not one of the 50 or so resumes that I read from the group had a reference to competitiveness. When I asked the group about this omission, the response was that they were afraid of seeming to "showy" or "conceited."

Big mistake.

Being able to perform well under pressure is a strong character trait. If you have it, you should let me know. Experience with team sports or team academic competitions are great character builders and great hooks for team-related interview questions.

This is not showy; it is good personal marketing.

- **Leadership roles:** Taking the initiative and creating a desired outcome is an important character trait, but be careful. I am not hiring you to be a leader. I am hiring you to be part of a team, and it will be a while before I need your leadership skills. It is good to know you have them, but if you cannot play other roles on a team, you probably will not work out in many corporate environments. Make sure that you include an equal amount of other team skills on your resume.

- **Multi-tasking:** I reviewed a resume for a family friend who was graduating from a nationally recognized university. She was concerned that her GPA at 3.1 was a little low and might diminish her opportunities. What struck me from my initial glance at her resume were all the activities in which she was involved. She must have had three or four extra-curricular activities going on at once. Wow, this girl could multi-task! Maybe NASA would not be a good fit for her, but her academic credentials coupled with her energy and drive created a very compelling skill-set. Not surprisingly, she found an internship in Washington, D.C., where these skills will come in handy.

The ability to multi-task is a skill in and of itself. If this is a strength of yours, make sure that your resume makes it clear with numerous examples.

- **Creativity:** Opportunities to illustrate creativity do not naturally flow from the strict rubric of a resume, but if you have a strong creative streak you should find an opportunity to show it. Painting or sculpting is interesting, but what I am really looking for is creative problem-solving. The context is not important. Creative people are creative in all aspects of their being so if you have a creative solution to a complex problem, no matter what the context, use it.

To test for creativity, I often will ask the following interview question, "Can you give me an example where you used your creativity to solve a problem in your everyday life?" 90% of the time I will get a blank stare, but one in ten interviewees will immediately get the question and come up with an interesting response.

My favorite response to this question went something like this:

> "Well, I like to drink a cup of hot tea in the morning, but if I make the tea when I first get up, it is cold by the time I'm through getting ready. If I make it afterwards, I have to waste time waiting for it to steep. However, through trial and error I determined the right temperature that I could begin steeping my tea when I first got up so it would be ready to drink when I was done getting ready."

This is obviously too trivial to include on a resume, but the point is worth repeating: Creative people tend to be creative in all aspects of their lives. I was pretty confident that this gentleman would apply the same logic to his work on my team. He did, by the way, for many years.

You may ask yourself why I would ask this question this way. If creative people tend to be creative in all aspects of their lives, why wouldn't I ask them a job-specific question? We will get into this in more detail later in the interview section, but my goal as an interviewer is to get at the passions of the interviewees to find out what makes them tick. In order to do that I have to get them out of their comfort zones and be assured that their answers are spontaneous and unrehearsed. This question will often accomplish this.

- **Organizational Skills**: Efficiency and productivity are necessities in a well-run business. If you have organized something such as an outing or event, list it. If you have managed a club or group of people, list it.

  Again, it is the skill that matters and may translate from one context to another.

Interests

You should reserve a line or two at the bottom of the page to list some of your interests. These make good hooks, but more important, they speak to your well-roundedness. If I hire you to work on my team, I will be spending a lot of time with you. It is much more enjoyable to hang around interesting people with common interests so be sure to list some interests.

However, avoid provocative declarations such as "avid Chicago Bears fan" or "enjoy right-wing politics." "Avid football fan" or "Chicago Bears fan" works just as well. As does "enjoy political debate" or "enjoy politics."

You have no idea who is going to be looking at your resume. It is better to articulate these passions in an interview when you have had an opportunity to size up the person on the other side of the table. If they are wearing a Rush Limbaugh button, go for it. Otherwise, avoid the risk.

Also, be prepared for the "Why" question: Why do you enjoy politics? Why are you so passionate about football? This is a perfect opportunity for you to redirect the conversation toward your passions. Make sure you know how to tie it in because the response, "I like to see people pound other people's heads in" as an answer to either question would not be productive!

Examples of what not to say on your resume *(and my sarcastic comments!)*

- Acquired strong communication and negotiation skills via dunning delinquent residential mortgagors over the phone

  Well, she is probably not exaggerating, but it also says something about her character that she was successful harassing and cajoling grandmothers to pay their late bills. Not sure I would suggest emphasizing this as a strength.

- Worked directly with the CEO, with primary responsibility for accuracy of inventory

  Not a good idea throwing titles around. Accuracy of inventory? Most CEOs are not "directly" involved in that.

- GPA 3.2908/4.000

  Oh, so close! I was looking for someone with a 3.2909. Sorry, but I'll have to put you in the reject pile.

- GPA: 3.8182/4.0

  So sloppy! It should be 3.8182/4.0000. Ahh, much better. Oh, by the way, you know what the difference is between the lifetime earnings stream of someone with a 3.8182 compared to 3.8? About as much as a cup of coffee at Wall Drugs. For those of you that have not travelled through the beautiful terrain of Eastern South Dakota, that's 10¢.

- Conducted independent market research project on groundbreaking prospective financial project

  You've got to break the ground first for it to be groundbreaking.

- Interests: Golfing, fishing, football, The Chicago Cubs, mixed martial arts, and weight lifting

  Oh no, a Cubs fan! Full of angst and envy; satisfied with mediocrity. A miserable lot we are. Big risk unless one is applying for a job at a tech support call center where getting yelled at and ridiculed is a daily staple. Just kidding, of course.

- Worked closely on projects with upper management, including the Chief Executive Officer, Vice President of …

  Whoop-tee-do. I once sat next to Nick Faldo on an airplane. Cannot say it improved my handicap. No mention of skills; no relevance.

- Interests: IM Sports, Bears fan, Monopoly enthusiast, and Spice Girls fanatic

  Spice Girls fanatic? There are some things you should keep to yourself.

- One of few to be invited back to conduct research with University professors in following summer's prestigious program, *Research in Biological Sciences 2*

  Sounds prestigious, especially the "2." Might have been more relevant if you told me about what applicable skills you learned.

Lifeguard
- Addressed customer concerns, resolved customer conflicts, and performed pool maintenance and cleaning
- Trained new lifeguards
- Monitored patron safety and enforced pool rules

  Well, I'll give him credit for this most eloquent description of a lifeguard's duties, but he was still just a lifeguard and not worthy of 3 bullets of precious real estate.

- One of 6 students selected to organize the International Pre-Orientation for 105 incoming first-year international students

  First, it should be "1 of 6" or "One of six"; and "international" is only needed once. Second, one of six out of how many total? I have no idea if this is selective or not, but more important, who cares?

XYZ Imports, CEO
- Founded an African art import company with over $400 in revenue

  "CEO" and "$400 in revenue" don't go together. One of the great things about being self-employed is that you can give yourself whatever title you want, but come on. You might think it sounds impressive, but I know better.

XYZ Corporation Inc., *Research Fellowship*– Chicago, IL   September 20xx–December 20xx

- Research and study the capital markets and the consultative process.
- Assist in the preparation and publishing of presentation materials for client and prospect meetings.
- Coordinate client and prospective client mailings and maintain appointment calendar.
- Arrange and initiate telephone contact with current and prospective clients.
- Prepare client portfolios and initiate contact with prospective clients.
- Assist with the planning of investment manager seminars and interactive conference calls.

When your action verbs are this weak, it should be a clue that there is too much detail. Notice, too, the small and irritating font.

Why do you think that she thinks that I care that she wrote stuff in a calendar, copied things, and called people?

VI. Interviewing

So far we have looked at cover letters and resumes and learned how to add a little shine to your presentation on paper. Now it is time to put this into three dimensions and focus on you: improving your appearance and performance in an interview.

Interviewing is one of the most nerve-wracking experiences that people face during our normal adult lives. Most of us (including me) are not very good at talking about ourselves and feel uncomfortable with complete strangers probing into our souls. Couple this with the fact that, more times than not, the outcome from your best efforts will be an ego-crushing "No" and you have a recipe for discomfort and stress.

Why is the interview process so problematic?

Scarcity of Data Problem and the Use of Heuristics

The first thing to realize is that until you become a seasoned professional, you will not have developed a reliable track record in a professional environment, and thus are a risky commodity for a hiring firm. I used to half-jokingly tell eager Goldman Sachs prospective hires that the best thing they could put on their resume to increase their chances of getting a job at Goldman Sachs was previous work experience at Goldman Sachs. The point being that known commodities carry less risk for an employer considering hiring them. It's a little bit like the chicken-and-egg problem. If you have the experience, then they know you can do it and will be more likely to want to hire you, but how do you get the experience in the first place?

So if you do not have a resume chock-full of relevant experiences, how are recruiters going to evaluate you? A common recruiting practice is to develop simple heuristics which attempt to map you to previous successes or failures. These heuristics many times focus on appearances and first impressions. They could be as simple—and arbitrary—as:

- He is slouching. Slouchers are not hard workers.
- She is fidgeting. Fidgeters don't work well in teams.
- His shirt is wrinkly. Poor physical appearance shows laziness and a lack of attention to detail.
- Nice smile. I bet she is a friendly team player.
- Very tidy suit and tie. This person looks like a winner.
- She said thank you when I opened the door for her. She is mature and thoughtful.

There are three key insights regarding the lack of good data and the use of heuristics. First, everyone you talk to will be using different heuristics, so it is impossible to know exactly what each interviewer will be focusing on, that is, there is a large part of the process you cannot control. Second, because of these different interpretations of your performance, heuristics are not as reliable as cold, hard facts and their use can lead to a much larger range of outcomes and more randomness to the interviewing experience. Much of this you also cannot control. Third, appearance and first impressions are very important. This you can influence. Learn to emulate other professionals and play to your interviewers' heuristics. Help them feel comfortable with you. This alone will not likely get you the job, but it can position you in the most favorable light and decrease the number of negative outcomes.

Inefficiency of Process

The second thing that makes the hiring process particularly difficult for first-time job seekers is that it is incredibly inefficient. Let's think about the typical on-campus recruiting event. You, the eager job seeker, have spent a fair amount of time and effort crafting and fine-tuning your resume and cover letter. You have overcome all the obstacles and uncertainties that we have already touched upon in just getting to the first round. Now, you will have approximately 20 minutes to sit down with a single representative from the hiring firm to state your case for getting the job. Your whole fate rests on the shoulders of this one person who may be your senior by only a few years.

What could go wrong? You might simply not hit it off with her. Your delivery could be flat and uninspirational. She might ask the wrong questions and completely miss your talents. You could stumble on one of the questions. You might make a joke that backfires. She might be in a bad mood or have something else on her mind and not really be focused on the interview. You might have bad breath or have scuffed shoes and set her heuristics off.

The point is that there are many different variables at play that determine the successes and failures in the interview process, many of which are outside of your control. Let's do a little exercise first and then focus on what you should do.

Fun with Numbers: What Is the Probability of Success?

Let's make a couple of simple assumptions and calculate what our chances of success are going into a first-round interview. Let's assume that 14 first-round candidates are selected and out of these 14, 3 get call-backs for second rounds. Of these 3, 1 is offered a job. That means $3/14 \times 1/3 = 1/14$ or just over 7% of those who make it to the interview process will get a job offer. You had a better chance of getting into Harvard than that! The Cubs even have a better chance of winning the World Series. Okay, maybe not, but you know what I mean.

There are two key points to take out of this little exercise. First, when conducting your job search, you have to be thinking about a multiple-firm strategy. Interviewing with three firms brings the odds up. Nine or ten will bring the odds up considerably. So don't take the attitude that you have to get a job at firm X and focus all of your efforts on that one opportunity. The second thing is that rejection is part of the process, so do not get uptight or think less of yourself. If you don't have immediate success, learn from your mistakes, refine your message, and keep going. Your persistence will pay off.

Persistence

Let me stress this last point. For many of you fresh college grads, up until this point in your lives you have had people doing a lot of things for you. Your life has been pretty much scripted, from taking the bus to school and soccer practice to taking courses you need to get your degree. The job search is a different ballgame. You have to do it yourself and work at it diligently. You have to go out and make it happen. It will define the rest of your life, more so than probably anything else that you have done so far. You have to be assertive and focused. You and only you can make it happen.

Tilting the Odds

What can you do to improve your odds of success in an interview? We have already discussed a number of points. By increasing the polish of your cover letter and resume, you have a better chance of being in the "likely" pile going into the interview.

Here are a number of key insights to further tilt the odds in your favor.

Before the Interview

- **Network:** Try to get to know as many people in the industry and firms in which you may be interested. It is never too early to start this process. Check your school's alumni database; contact friends of your family. You may be surprised how many people will be eager to share with you their insights and experiences.

  If you can get a personal recommendation, you become a known quantity and your risk level drops precipitously. However, this should not be your main objective; it is simply to learn as much about the culture and mores of the firms as you can in order to play to your future interviewers' heuristics.

- **Gain familiarity with the job and job environment:** Visit as many job sites that you can. Try to determine what the people in the positions that you are applying to actually do. This will make your interview answer sound much more knowledgeable. Observe what people are wearing, their mannerisms, and their demeanor, and emulate them.

  You will not only improve your interview performance, but you will also get a better understanding of what jobs might be a good fit for your skill set. Could you do, or would you like to do, what they do? Would you want to be like them?

- **Research:** Make sure that you are familiar with the current news and, if possible, the strategic plan of the firm. This type of information is usually discussed at the analysts' call after each quarterly earnings report and should be on the firm's Web site. It is silly, but a number of people will ask you if you know what the company's current stock price is as an indication of your interest, so be prepared.

- **Practice:** You want your delivery in the interview to be fluid but not scripted. Practice the night before how you might answer different questions (a long list follows below), but do not memorize your answers. Also, if you have not had an interview in a couple of weeks, ask a friend or relative to give you a mock interview so you can keep your delivery and timing sharp. Go over possible interview questions in your head. Refrain from overconfidence. You will be kicking yourself if you are thrown off-guard by a question you should have been able to answer.

- **Appearance:** Make sure your interview suit is clean and you have a nicely pressed shirt and shining shoes. Get a good night's sleep and go get 'em!

Presentation / First Impressions

As I mentioned earlier, first impressions are very important. This is especially true for young and inexperienced prospective hires. You do not, by nature, have many data points for a would-be employer to look to as evidence that you will be a successful worker. Employers must judge this from every piece of evidence they can find. First impressions may set this off in the right or wrong direction.

How do you make a good first impression? Do you give your interviewer a firm handshake and a slap on the back? Do you tell a funny joke to break the ice? Do you try to avoid eye contact if at all possible and slink into the room silently?

Of course, none of the above would be appropriate. Let's go through the basics:

- **Be on time:** If you make me wait, you start in a big hole. It happens, right? Even the most punctual people are occasionally late, but unfortunately, I don't know you well enough to know if this is a rare occurrence or the norm. I am likely to assume the latter. Being on time means planning to be there early!

What should you do if you are late? As in most other cases, I will advise you to show maturity and address this issue head-on. This means that you admit to it and apologize for making your interviewer wait. Here are some bad excuses:

o "I did not think it would take me this long to get here."
o "My alarm did not go off."
o "Wow, I cannot believe I spaced it!"
o "No one told me it would take me so long to get through the building security."

Well, my response to these excuses is: If you thought working for my team was important, you should have planned better. Don't go there.

What defines late? If I am ready to talk with you and you are not, then you are late. It does not matter if it is ten seconds or ten minutes. You are late.

Let's face it: With modern technology, you should never, ever make someone wait. If you think you may be late, don't risk it; call or email them and let them know that you have been detained. Given 15 minutes notice, most people will willingly tweak their schedules to be accommodating.

If for whatever reason you are late or detained in some other way, you should realize at this point that you have made a bad first impression and need to immediately and aggressively try to dispel your interviewers' probable interpretation that you are lazy and irresponsible. If you have a reasonable excuse, give it to them. As long as you don't whine and say something like the excuses above, it might help. Either way, you need to give me some evidence from previous experience that you are not a slacker to help mend this first impression: perfect attendance in high school, swam laps every morning, etc.

Remember that before you walk into the room, I have probably already placed you in the "likely" or "not likely" category. If you are in the "not likely" camp then probably nothing you say at this point will matter, but if you are in the "likely" group, then you just might be able to convince me that this was just a fluke.

- **Dress appropriately:** In finance, a conservative grey or dark blue suit, white or light blue shirt or blouse (and silk tie for men) are standard protocol for your interview. Pant suits are fine for women. Other industries may be different. Make sure you know beforehand what is appropriate attire. Your suit should be tailored. Don't balk at the price. Some of you will have spent upward of a quarter of a million dollars on your college education. If a primary reason for your education is to get a good job, $300 to $500 for a nice suit and a couple of all-cotton shirts and silk ties is a great value. Make sure your shirts are nicely pressed. Please wear socks and nice shoes. I will notice all these details. Any aberration from normal will cause me to question subconsciously whether you will fit into my team.

  Smart business attire will give you confidence and put you on the same sartorial stature as your interviewer. Many firms now allow casual attire. Do you still have to wear a business suit? If in doubt, the answer is yes. You can always ask the human resources personnel what is proper attire for the interview. If you are underdressed you will lose confidence in yourself and will not make a good impression.

  o Hide all tattoos and body piercings. You are free to your own form of self-expression after work hours but not during.
  o Women: Don't wear heavy perfume or excessive makeup. Eye shadow to match your blue shirt might not go over well. Many of the interviewing rooms are quite small; a heavy dose of perfume will linger for hours and leave a literal bad taste in my mouth.
  o Guys: Please shower and shave. Fresh breath is appreciated.

Treat ALL employees with courtesy and mutual respect: I was blessed to have one of the best administrative assistants in the business. I found early on that some people treated me quite differently than they treated her. She would tip me off about these individuals. Her input could have a major impact on a candidate's chances.

Every interaction with every person at a firm that you are trying to get a job at is important. If a "lowly" administrative assistant or human resource person calls or emails you, you should have the same promptness and professionalism as if the CEO of the company was expecting a reply. If he or she gets you a cup of coffee or glass of water, say "thank you." You just don't know. It may very well be that my first impression of you is from my assistant. If she tells me that you were difficult to deal with or impolite, I will frame your initial candidacy in this light.

Besides, being courteous and treating all people with respect is a strong character trait. It shows a high sense of self-confidence and internal direction. It shows a person who has visited and understands the teaching of the Oracle. Give it a try!

- **Greet with confidence:** Your handshake should be firm but not excessive. Make eye contact at the time of the handshake. It seems silly, but it makes a good impression. Smile if it helps you relax. If there is some dead time between the initial greeting and the start of the interview, don't feel obligated to make any small talk. If you have a walk to the interview room or are waiting for an additional interviewer to arrive, let the other lead. If he or she chooses silence, reciprocate.

- **Position yourself appropriately:** When entering the interviewing room, wait for instructions as to where to sit. Some people are particular and you want to make sure that your interviewer is comfortable and focused.

During the Interview

- **Maintain eye contact with the interviewer:** Not a piercing, continuous stare or an occasional glance, but something in between. When being spoken to, show total engagement. You want your eyes to show how interested you are working for my team. Practice this.

- **Sit up straight:** You want to be on the front of your chair looking highly engaged and aggressive. Don't fidget or tap your finger or pen.

- **Maintain a professional demeanor:** When we are nervous, we can show some bad habits. Don't finish my sentences for me or interrupt me. Say "thank you" if I open the door for you and "please" if you would like something to drink. Refrain from colloquialism and slang. Don't get too relaxed. An interview is no place for backslapping and jokes. Only use my first name if I tell you it is okay to do so.

- **Don't be too causal:** Some interviewers will try to catch you off guard by trying to make you feel too comfortable and treat you like a buddy or old friend. For some, this is an innocent technique to help you relax. Some are more devious and are trying to make you slip up and say something you may regret. In either case, don't mistake "friendly" with "friend." You should reciprocate and mimic their friendly demeanor, but you should not treat them like a buddy or an old friend. They are not.

  There are certain things that you tell your buddies that you should not mention in an interview. For instance, if an interviewer says something like, "Boy, I hated going to class" or "Boy, I hope you don't party as much as I did at school," he or she is probably not trying to bond with you, but more likely is trying to uncover a weakness in your character. She may be leading you down a dangerous path. Don't follow. Notice that neither of the above statements are real questions. They do not require a real answer. A friendly chuckle or a smile will do.

  Likewise, don't cross the "good buddy" line unprovoked. Just because I may be the same gender as you does not mean that you can behave like we are in a barroom pounding some cold ones. The only time "hot" and "woman" should be in the same sentence is if you are talking about a medical condition. Likewise, if you utter the word "chick" it had better be in connection with a reflection of a kindergarten project. I think you get the idea.

- **Don't be too colloquial:** Slang or regional or generational phrases should be avoided.

- **Don't slouch, rock, or recline:** From our earlier discussion on heuristics it should be clear why this is important. Your posture will impact my perception of you. Slouchers come across as passive and unfocused, rockers (and tappers) as nervous and high-maintenance, recliners as self-centered and poor team players. You want to look eager and aggressive. During the first 80% of the interview, no part of your back should be touching the back of your chair. You want to create the impression that if I ask you to do something for me, you will jump at the opportunity. When it is your turn to ask questions you can relax a little, but not before.

- **Answer the question:** Not answering the question that is asked is a common mistake of even seasoned interviewees. In an interview this is much harder than it sounds. I will often ask a simplistic question, such as "Name x number of your personal strengths" or "What are the x most interesting places you have visited?" to see if the interviewee can follow specific directions and only name x. A productive worker needs to understand what is being asked of him and execute his tasks effectively. Properly answering an interview question reveals this quality.

- **Bring something to drink:** An interview is a very nerve-wracking experience. Many people will develop a dry mouth. I have had poor souls develop a clicking sound in their throats as they struggle to continue talking. It is hard to recover from this in a 25-minute interview, so it is best to come prepared.

- **Relax!** You will do fine.

Know Yourself Cold

Your resume, cover letter, and any other information you present about yourself and your achievements should be factual and defendable. Most well-run companies will do an extensive background check on recently hired candidates and have been known to rescind offers when they find inaccurate information. Case in point: A candidate to whom I had extended an offer had inaccurately reported the dates during which he had been enrolled at a university, completing his Ph.D. The amount of time in question was less than one year, but to my human resources department this was grounds to void his offer letter. I had to intercede to save his candidacy, which I gladly did, but the point is that with a lack of reliable data about you, one inaccuracy, even an innocent mistake, can have a significant implication.

Equally important, you need to be able to support and defend every word on your resume. I have stressed many times that it is invaluable to get others to read and critique your resume and cover letters, but you are the one who will need to articulate what is on the paper during the interview. Don't let others wordsmith your resume to the point where you do not feel comfortable with the end result. I have also stressed the importance of including relevant coursework and research that you have completed to create hooks to help lead the interviewer to your strengths, but be careful. You must be prepared to answer detailed questions about anything on your resume. More than once I have had interviewees who could not recall a project or a work experience that they referenced on their resumes. Something you cannot recall in detail does not make a valuable hook. You are being misleading and showing poor judgment if you list a relevant course or experience but cannot defend it!

Moreover, be careful with including superlatives such as "superior," "excellent," and "excelled" on your resume unless you can vigorously defend their use. You may think that you have superior skills because you received an "A" or even an "A+" in a particular course. However, I will be comparing your skills to a wider universe of talent, and your word choice might seem to me to be an embellishment and a violation of the wisdom of the Oracle. For instance, you might think that you have superior communication skills because you consistently get excellent marks in your English and writing courses and thus you feel justified in using the phrase "excellent communication skills." However, when I think of "excellent" communication skills, I think of someone who has the ability to articulate positions clearly and to persuade others to adopt their own point of view; or someone who feels comfortable giving a speech to a room full of 400 people. Needless to say, when I ask you why you would rate your communication skills as excellent, your answer needs more to it than "I got good grades in English."

By the way, I love to challenge people who have these superlatives on their resumes because it is such an easy way for me to find out if someone has visited the Oracle. Sometimes I do this because it reconfirms my negative impression of them, and I can quickly determine their fate. However, I am occasionally surprised and someone pulls it off. They actually can support and defend such a lofty adjective. These people make a lasting impression.

So here is the dilemma: If you are an expert you want me to know it, because it is a valuable skill that may help you get the job. However, if you say and think you are an expert but you are not, you are doomed. 99 times out of 100, those applying for entry-level positions fall in this category, so do us both a favor and don't try to describe yourself as such. Focus on articulating your deeds and accomplishments as best you can and let me come up with my own label to match what I hear. At this stage, I am looking more for potential rather than mastery. Don't shoot yourself in the foot by trying to portray yourself as something more than you are.

Last, practice answering questions about yourself. You know by now how to study for a test. An interview is no different. You would never take an important test "cold." Why would you even think about going into an interview without reviewing your notes and re-reading your study material?

Follow Instructions

What a lot of young interviewees don't realize is that many times the interviewer is not as interested in what you say as in how you say it. One of the important things that I look for in an interview is how well a candidate can understand what I am asking and can stay on task while answering it. If I ask you to name your top strength and biggest weakness, I am asking for *one* of each. Just one. Do I care what these answers are? Yes, I do, but I am also testing you to see how well you follow instructions. Members of my team who can listen to what I want and execute effectively are extremely valuable. Too often, interviewees will over-answer the question and ramble on about things that they think are important; unfortunately, often these things are not relevant to the question I have asked. This tendency reveals a candidate to be a high-maintenance employee, which I do not need.

Often, I like to ask a general question such as the one above with the intent to ask a second more detailed follow-up question. For instance, if your response to the question above was that your top strength was your ability to work in a team, then I am likely to ask you a question that explores this strength, for example, "Tell me about a team that you worked in which you thought worked particularly well and why?" If you answered the initial question that you like working in teams, have strong analytical skills, are a strong leader, are a good listener, have a voracious appetite for knowledge, have a strong competitive streak, are a self-starter, and have strong ethics and moral fiber, and so on, you have thrown me so many pieces of data that I am apt to miss the mark on my follow-up question and may ask about one of your least impressive strengths.

Probably the number one thing that loses my interest in a candidate more than any other is when he starts rambling. Answer the specific question asked. Don't assume you know better than I do what I should be asking. I will get there if I think it is relevant.

If you really want to elaborate or expand upon the question, ask me if it is okay. This shows a sense of maturity and respect, for example, "I have two strengths that I believe are equally important. Would you mind if I mentioned both of them?" Wow, you have just politely and effectively moved the discussion in a way that benefits your candidacy without usurping control of the interview. You might be just what I need to round out my team!

Staying on Cue

What happens if you don't understand the question that is being asked or, even worse, halfway into your brilliant monologue, you have forgotten what the question was? If this has not happened to you yet, it will. It happens to all of us. Don't panic. Here are some tips on how to recover from these situations.

The first one is easy. If you do not understand the question, ask for clarification. This is perfectly fine. If someone asked you if you dealt with ABC agreement or XYZ procedures, and you don't know what these are, say so. We interviewers are far from perfect; we might have introduced some very specific knowledge that is rightly over your head. Or, perhaps we are a little devious and are purposely asking you a question that you probably do not know to see how you will react. Saying, "I don't know" is okay. Don't try to answer a different question or say you know something that you don't. You should know by now why this is problematic.

The second case is a little more difficult to deal with, and surprisingly it happens quite often. If you forget the question, most people's response is to ramble on, thinking that they can buy time and perhaps remember the question. It is a much more mature response to pause and confess: "I am sorry. I seem to have gotten a little lost in my response. Have I adequately answered your question?" or "My apologies. I have gotten a little off track. What was it exactly that you wanted me to answer?" You can usually get away with this at least once during the interview.

In either case, coming clean and risking making yourself look unimpressive in the eyes of your interviewer is the right move. It shows maturity, self-confidence, and superior judgment. Yes, your run the risk of the interviewer thinking that you should have known something that you didn't, but the alternative risks inherent in rambling and embellishing the truth are worse.

Repeating the Question

The best defense against losing your train of thought is to avoid getting yourself into this situation in the first place. A little tip I recommend to my students is to repeat the question after it has been asked. For example, if an interviewer asks you, "What where the two most interesting team exercises that you experienced in your summer internship?" You would respond, "My two most interesting team experiences over the summer were…" The advantage of this rote exchange is threefold. First, it buys you a little extra time to organize your thoughts and formulate your response. Second, it allows your brain to hear the question one more time and perhaps make it stick. Third, it is guaranteed to start your response moving in the right direction.

Also, make sure you practice making short, insightful responses. A good interviewer will try to ask you a question in a way that you have not heard before to see if you can think on your feet The more often you mentally practice different responses ahead of time, the easier you will be able to put these together in a meaningful way to answer anything the interviewer can throw at you.

Delivering Your Message

Some interviewees are advised to be aggressive and to take charge of the interview: no matter what the initial question, hit the interviewer with your greatest selling points to create the right first impression. This is counter-intuitive if you think about it. If I am interviewing you, I am hiring you to work for me and to take directions from me; why on earth would it make a good first impression on me that you didn't answer the questions that I ask? I think it is a serious mistake to try to explicitly lead the interview. If you try, you are likely to be seen as egotistical and a poor team player and might be earmarked in that dreaded category of "high maintenance."

100

There are much more effective ways to sell yourself and to direct the interview in a way that puts you in the best light. The first one is something we have mentioned many times already and that is the effective placement of hooks throughout your resume and cover letter. An effective hook will grab the interviewer's eyes and help them formulate the questions that will highlight your strengths. Hooks can also be employed during an interview in your responses to general interview questions.

I have a series of topics that I like to cover in an interview. The topics vary with the position and the level of experience of the candidate, but in general I try to touch on the following: Intellectual capacity, teamwork, creativity, taking the initiative, competitiveness, knowledge of the particular job, or interest in the particular field. I don't, however, have a set script. I like to start out with a general question as an introduction and give the interviewee a chance to direct the interview in the direction that he or she wants. Then, I ask specific follow-up questions. For example, an interview could start something like this:

Scott: "Tell me about your summer experience working for XYZ corporation?"

Interviewee: "I was on a great team and learned a lot about the pressures of working in a fast-paced environment. I also had the ability to take the initiative and develop some creative solutions to some interesting client-driven problems."

There is so much meat in that response. I could drill down in a number of ways:

Scott: "Interesting. Why would you say that your team was great?"

Or

Scott: "What did you like about working in a pressure-packed environment? What did you learn about yourself?"

Or

Scott: "Can you give me a couple of examples of where you used your own initiative to solve a client-related problem?"

Compare the richness of the follow-up questions with that of a much more specific response to the initial question:

Scott: "Tell me about your summer experience working for XYZ Corporation?"

Interviewee: "The area that I worked in was responsible for developing solutions to customer problems. I did a lot of spreadsheet and database work and answered customer calls and helped solve their problems."

My follow up questions may not be as deep and meaningful:

Scott: "Can you tell me about some to the tools you used in your spreadsheet work?"

Or

Scott: "What were some of the problems you helped solve?"

There are a few important takeaways from this sample conversation. First, you can implicitly lead the interview by framing your responses to general questions to highlight what you want to talk about, i.e. your strengths. Second, you want to match the specificity of your answer with that of the question. That is, answer general questions with general responses and specific questions with specific responses. Third, as always, practice being concise and answering the question that is asked.

Commonly Asked Interview Topics and Questions

Academic Excellence / Continual Learning

- What was your favorite class and why?
- What academic achievement are you most proud of?
- What is the most interesting book that you have read lately?
- What class have you recently taken that you found particularly challenging?
- What class unrelated to your major did you take just for fun?

Being a Team Player

- Tell me about a team that you worked on that you think functioned particularly well, and why?
  - What role did you play on this team?
  - How did you contribute to its success?
- Tell me about a team that you worked on that you think functioned poorly, and why?
  - What did you do to try to improve its functioning?
  - What did you learn from this experience?
- What types of roles (such as leader) do you like to play on teams?
- What is the optimal size for a team?
- What does it mean to be a good team player?
- Do you consider yourself to be a good team player? If so, why?

Competitiveness

- Do you consider yourself to be a competitive person?
- Give me an example that illustrates your competitiveness.
- Give me an example where the odds were against you, but you refused to give up and turned a negative experience into a positive one.

Initiative

- Give me an example of when you took the initiative to solve a difficult problem.
- Tell me about the team / club / business that you started and why.

- Do you consider yourself a self-starter? Give me a couple of examples that illustrate this skill.

Multi-tasking

- Can you give me an example of when you had multiple assignments due simultaneously and what you did to get them all completed?
- Give me an example of when you were faced with a deadline where you did not have adequate time to get everything done. What did you do?

Creativity

- Do you consider yourself a creative person?
- Can you give me an example where you used your own creativity to solve a problem?

Knowledge of a Particular Job / Firm

- What does it mean to be a successful analyst / salesperson / clerk / ...?
  - Which of these skills would you consider strengths?
  - Which of these skills would you consider you are least apt at?
- Can you give me an example or two of related work you have done?
- From what you know about my firm, how would you describe its culture?
- What is the current stock price of my company?
- What have you read recently about my company?

Interest in a Particular Field

- What interests you about finance / banking / marketing ...?
- What are the skills that you think are necessary to be successful in the field?
  - Which one of these would you consider your greatest strength?
  - Which one would you consider your least greatest strength?
- Can you give me an example of a project that you have worked on that you think the skills you learned are directly related to this position?
- How do you feel your educational experience has prepared you for a job in...?
- How do you feel your past work experience and extra-curricular activities have prepared you for a job in ...?
- What other types of jobs/industries are you looking at? How does this position compare to those?

- Where do you want to be in 5 / 10 years? How do you see this position moving you in that direction?
- What are your life goals? How do you think a career in (this field) will help you achieve these goals?

Ethics

- Have you ever found yourself in an ethical dilemma? What did you do to resolve it?
- If you uncovered a situation where a co-worker had improperly billed a customer / was involved in an illegal activity / had divulged proprietary information, what would you do?

Risk Taking / Judgment

- Do you consider yourself a risk taker?
- Give me an example of when you took an appropriate risk.
- Give me an example of when you took a risk and it did not work out for you.
  - What did you learn?
- Give me example of a class or project you have undertaken that is the least related to your major. What motivated you to take it?
- Have you ever travelled to a different culture? What did you learn about yourself and your own country?
- Tell me about the most interesting place you have visited and why.

Miscellaneous

- What do you like to do for fun?
- Tell me something about yourself that is not on your resume.
- Who do you most admire and why?
- If you could meet any person alive or dead, who would it be? What would you ask him or her?
- What has been the greatest challenge or adversity in your life? What did you do to overcome it?
- What are your life goals outside of your career?
- At your funeral, what would you hope that people will say about you?

VII.   Career Choices: Narrowing Down the Opportunity Set

In reviewing techniques to improve your interviewing skills, resumes, and cover letters, the focus has been on presenting your candidacy in the best possible light. We have stressed eliminating riskiness in your presentation and expressing yourself in a direct, concise, and skill-based way that will help your would-be employer hone in on your strengths and allow you to express your character and capacity.

This next chapter focuses on determining what types of firms will be the best fit for your personality. Finding a role that matches your skill set will increase your chances of excelling at your job, but joining an organization that fits your way of thinking and personal ethics is equally important to your chances of success. Even more important, your choice may influence your quality of life more than almost anything else.

Understanding the personality of the firms on your target list should be integrated with your job search and should not be left to chance.

Embracing the Free Market

In many respects a job search is no different from any other economic transaction. You, the job seeker, are the seller of your human capital; the employer is the buyer. Yes, you as the seller could do such a good job at selling that the employer buys based on heightened expectations. But remember that with any product, if it does not live up to expectation, it will be returned or discarded and replaced by another product that better meets the expectation of the buyer. Thus, the best salesperson is the one who is able to understand his or her product and find those buyers that can best benefit from its use, and then best articulate accurate selling points. The honest, thoughtful salesman may lose some initial sales, but will create trust within the marketplace and will be rewarded in the long run.

Your job search is no different. Your skills and passions are your product, and either they "fit" with the particular role and particular firm, or they don't. Overselling yourself into a role or career path that is not a good "fit" may lead to instant gratification and the admiration of your peers, but it is not the recipe for long-term success. Don't fight or try to outsmart the free market. Embrace it and let it guide you on your journey.

- **Be open and honest:** This is why I have stressed throughout this book to be open and honest, not only with yourself, but with your perspective employers. Remember the teaching of the Oracle: Know thyself. Your starting point for narrowing down your career directions starts here. Go back and skim Chapter I if this concept is not fresh in your mind.

  The ability to understand and articulate your passions is essential for the free market to work and to place you in a position—and on a career path—that will lead to success and intellectual and spiritual fulfillment. These concepts are linked; it is very hard to have one without the other.

- **Explore all interesting opportunities:** When you are at the beginning of your job search, you should be open to all interesting opportunities that present themselves. This is part of exploring your passions and understanding where your strengths lie. Sample the free market and find out the value of these different opportunities. If you were to send a cover letter and resume articulating your skills and passions to firms in 10 different industries, you are sampling the free market. If 9 of the 10 do not respond positively, then the free market is providing evidence that these may not be good fits for your career direction. If one replies back affirmatively, then the free market is telling you that there may be some interested buyers for your skill set in that area and you should explore a little deeper.

  The corollary is also true. If you are focused on one particular market segment and you have been openly and honestly selling yourself but you are not finding any interested buyers, then perhaps you should be shopping your wares elsewhere. If you take a skills-based approach to your career development, you will be able to get where you most want to go from many different starting points.

- **Don't be ideological or inflexible:** Being honest and willing to explore an array of possible opportunities does not mean you should be inflexible if an opportunity arises that is good, but not perfect. Your focus should be on developing the skills that push you in the general direction of your passions. Don't pass on an opportunity because it is not exactly right. You will have plenty of opportunities to straighten your course. Keep your eye on the goal line, and if the opportunity that is in front of you will move you in that direction, you should seriously consider it. I want to stress your job search is not an ideological pursuit. It is a calculated exercise, the goal of which is to make you a productive member of society. In the end, you may have to take whatever the free market pushes your way. A bird in the hand is worth two in the bush!

- **Focus on developing skills:** Each step along your career path should be focused on developing skills that allow you to express your passions. Each step allows you to express them a little more or in a different way. At some point in your career, you may have to compromise your passions a bit to meet some shorter-term monetary or family goals. This is common in most career progressions, but this is not something that a first-time job seeker should worry about. You should have an understanding of your long-term goals and the necessary skills to reach them, and evaluate career opportunities with respect to whether they help you to obtain those skills.

Say, for instance, you have a passion for linguistic self-expression, i.e. you have an outgoing personality and you enjoy socializing, intellectual debate, and thinking quickly on your feet. Should you take the high-powered-number-crunching financial analyst position at a big brand investment bank or the multi-tasking-roll-up-your-sleeves public relations analyst job at the no name social service organization? There is no question that the latter is a much better fit for you and will allow you to better develop the skills that feed your passions.

When confronted with this choice in the abstract, some people get it right and say that they would take the public relations role, but in reality most people would go the other way. The allure of the high-paying big brand is too overwhelming. They will initially feel good about their decision because of the lauds and admiration of their peers, but they will probably have the worst two years of their lives. Perhaps they will get lucky and be able to transfer over to a public relations or marketing position within the big brand firm; numerous internal opportunities are one of the advantages of working for large firms. However, most likely they will be trapped in a role that is not a good fit and will not be moving in a direction that is consistent with their long-term goals.

Think twice about making this common mistake. Don't sacrifice your long-term goals for short-term gains. It usually is not worth it.

The Meaning of Life

It all comes down to this:

> ***From your understanding of your passions, you want to establish LIFE goals. You want to develop skills that lead to the expression of these passions, and your short-term decisions and the steps along your career path should be weighed with your long-term LIFE goals and expectations in mind.***

What do I mean by life goals? This is a broad and philosophical topic. See Stephen Covey, the self-help guru and author of *7 Habits of Highly Effective People*, for a fuller explanation, but basically the idea is to figure out where you want to end up and work backwards. Start by asking yourself: "Where do I want to go with my life?" "What do I hope to accomplish?" I am not talking about how much money you are going to make or where you want to retire, but the skills that you want to obtain, the impact that you hope to make, and how you want to be remembered.

You might not be able to fully articulate your life goals just yet and that is okay. As long as you seek experiences and acquire skills that move you in the general direction of expressing your passions, you will not be working against them and will continually be gaining more insight into their true nature.

- **Achieving success and finding out where you excel:** Success is highly correlated with those who have found a way to fully express their passions. People who are expressing their passions excel at what they are doing. They are also generally content with their lives.

  Happiness is not normally mentioned in the recruiting process or the business world, in general, but it is extremely important and is one of the implicit goals of your career path. Doing what you excel at will lead to your success and it will also likely lead to a happy and fulfilled life. But don't get this mixed up. It is not the success that will make you happy nor will happiness make you successful. It is the expression of your passions that is the underlying driver for both.

Work Environment

As I outlined above, the secret to career success and happiness is to fully express your passions, but in order to do this you must be in an environment that enables this. Every firm has its own identity. Your goal in your job search is not only to find a job where you can develop the skills that lead to the expression of your passions, but also to find an environment which is conducive to this growth.

Small Versus Large Firms

Let's first take a broad brush and discuss the differences between small and large firms. Small and large in this context can roughly be delineated between privately held and publicly traded companies. As we will discuss shortly, every firm has its own personality, but there are some distinctions we can draw at this broad level. Both can provide excellent starting points for one's career, but offer different positive and negatives.

Positives

Large firms can usually offer a more formal training and mentoring program. This may be an important criterion for a new member of the work force. Along with these training opportunities, they often offer multiple career paths. As one becomes comfortable with the work environment, there may be multiple chances to explore and find the opportunities that best hit your passions. Large firms also offer a marquee name that may help you during subsequent job searches. You are a known quantity.

In contrast, small firms have the advantage in flexibility and the ability for more self-expression. It is much easier to have your talents stand out and to gain recognition. There is also usually more opportunity for multi-tasking: doing many different activities instead of focusing on one main task. Finally, because of their less formal structure, small firms often offer quicker advancement into management and leadership positions.

Negatives

On the negative side, large firms tend to be bureaucratic and hierarchical. If a large firm claims to have a flat organizational structure, don't believe it. There is no such thing for any firm, beyond one run by a sole proprietor. A firm has either an implicit or explicit hierarchy. In an explicit hierarchy, power and control is managed through titles and organizational charts; in an implicit hierarchy, power and control rests in individual people. Those firms that claim to have a flat organizational structure are confusing "flat" with an implicit hierarchy. All firms must have a hierarchy, or they would be unmanageable. Large firms have multiple layers to their hierarchies, which makes it difficult for the firm's leaders to know who are the most talented and highest potential junior level employees. Because of this, perceptions and political positioning can be as important as personal talent in determining career success. This can be especially true for firms with implicit hierarchy. Understanding and catering to the sources of power within the organization can often be an important "skill" in advancing in a large firm.

Small firms have their downside, too. They do not always have the most well-defined career paths. Sometimes it can be difficult to understand where you may head after you have mastered your current role. Moreover, many times the personality of a small firm is dictated by the personality of one individual. Your personal advancement could be tied to whether you think like her or are in her good graces. Small firms generally do not have as many resources to focus on managing and mentoring new employees, nor do they always have adequate resources to solve employee grievances and to address work-related issues.

This is a gross simplification of how firms differ, but the important point is that firm size does matter, and understanding how you may fare in the different environments is important for narrowing down your opportunity set. If you feel that you need more structure at this stage of your career or don't have a good idea of exactly what you might want to do, then you may want to gravitate toward larger firms. On the other hand, if you love to multi-task and are comfortable in an environment that may not be well-defined, then a small firm perhaps would offer you the best growth opportunities.

Again, if you feel that a smaller firm might be a better fit but you have received a compelling job offer from a large firm (or vice versa), be practical. By all means, take it. At this stage of your career, you are looking to acquire skills that lead to the expression of your passions, and this will send you in that direction.

Corporate Cultures

Firms are like people: each one has its own unique personality, mores, and ethos, and after you have worked in one for a while, you begin to adopt these traits as well. If the firm's characteristics are consistent with your own, then this will be a good thing and you will revel in the "fit." Your association with your company will be a source of happiness and pride. It will be a fertile ground for socializing and friendship; it will become the centerpiece of your life. Moreover, you will be content with your career growth. You will feel that you are making strides in reaching your passions and continue to gain confidence in your abilities.

If it is a bad fit, then the opposite may happen. You will find that you don't really fit in, and though you try to befriend your cohorts, you will find that you don't really have much in common with them. Though you try to adapt and think like the others think, you will keep encountering inconsistencies with your own personal mores and this creates anxiety and displeasure. You will also find that others tend to be advancing quicker than you, and you will begin to question your own capabilities.

All this disparity because of a difference in corporate fit? You bet! It can make a big difference. Think about the different college choices, or even majors, that you explored. How would your opportunity set have been different had you chosen a different path? Now multiply that by ten and you are in the ballpark of the impact that finding a firm with the right corporate culture for you will have.

We can tend to be like the frog placed in the pot to boil when it comes to our current jobs. As it gets hotter and hotter we continue to swim around knowing something is wrong, but fearing that the uncertainty of change might be even worse. Few of us are acute enough to realize a bad situation and quickly extricate ourselves from it. Instead we tend to wallow around in it until the pain and discomfort becomes unbearable.

The best way to avoid getting into a bad corporate fit is to do your homework ahead of time and focus your job search on those companies that you think you may fit well in.

How do you find out if you are good "fit"? Again, you first must know yourself and have visited the Oracle to understand the mores and ethos that you value in a culture. Next, you have to ascertain what traits are valued by each firm. How do you do this?

Most companies will have a mission statement and a section on their Web site that speaks directly about their culture. A lot of times these are blatant sales pitches, but sometimes you can glean some interesting aspects about a company. Asking about the culture of a company is always a very thoughtful question to ask during an interview. This is especially true during a second-round interview when you are speaking with a number of different people. Asking each person you talk to will provide you with a good picture of what it is really like to work there. By networking and meeting people at different companies in a non-interview setting, you will tend to get more realistic responses. Are the people you meet like you? Are they intellectually stimulating? Are they passionate about what they are doing? Would you enjoy being around them five days a week, eight or more hours a day?

When you have the opportunity to visit an office of a prospective employer, you should absorb as much information as possible. What traits does the culture stress? How are the work environments organized? Are most people working in offices behind closed doors, or are they in cubes with many opportunities for interactions? How casual is the dress? Are people in business attire or jeans? Are people punctual and friendly, or are they uptight and anxious? You can pick up many subtle clues from these observations and begin to get a good sense of whether or not you feel you fit in.

Would someone really make a career decision based on a company's culture? I did. Four years out from college, the company I worked for ceased operations. I was fortunate to have three very compelling job offers. Two had a better overlap with my current skill set, while the third was not as strong, but had a culture and work environment that was a strong fit. I chose the one with the greatest fit. It was the smartest thing I ever did!

Afterword

From the Oracle of Delphi to the Meaning of Life

I hope you have enjoyed the odyssey of exploration that this book has taken you on. You may have figured out by now that *enjoyment in seeing others learn* is a passion of mine, and that writing this book and making a meaningful impact in some unique way are on my list of life goals. I can now tick those off and go on to the next ones.

We are never really able to completely finish something when it touches our passions, and are always looking for opportunities to express them further, so I am sure that there will be some follow-up work in the future. We can always dig deeper into corporate culture, life goals, and success stories of those who have followed their passions. I would also love to help the interviewer and resume and cover letter readers. Many of them need as much help as the first-time job seekers.

I will continue to learn from my current students and refine the core concepts of *Polished* for years to come. In this same vein, I am anxious to hear from you. If there is something you liked or didn't like about the book, something that should be added or deleted, or something that you did not fully understand, please drop me a line. I cannot guarantee that I can personally respond to each inquiry, but I will certainly try.

Finally, if you want to give it a go and add polish to your resume, cover letter, or interviewing skills, I wish you the best of luck. I also offer you my personal services. Please check out my Web site for details.

Follow your passions. I look forward to learning about your future successes!

R. Scott Morris
President
Morris Consulting, LLC
scott@PolishedU.com
www.PolishedU.com

P.S. If you have any funny resume or cover letter stories to add to my "Examples of what not to say..." sections please forward them on – along with your own sarcastic comments, of course!

About The Author

R. Scott Morris

Career Highlights:

- President, Morris Consulting, LLC
- CEO, Boston Options Exchange Group, LLC
- Managing Director, Goldman Sachs and Company
- Partner, Hull Trading Company

Other Activities:

- Lecturer, University of Chicago, Chicago Careers in Business Program
- Guest Lecturer, Carnegie Mellon, Computational Finance Program
- Chair, Hinsdale Caucus
- Member, University of Chicago Visiting Committee

Education:

- University of Chicago, MBA, Finance and Statistics
- University of Chicago, AB, Economics

Interests:

- Golf, Baseball, Wine

Scott has over twenty years experience in the financial services industry. He has always been very active in the hiring and recruiting process. He has reviewed thousands of resumes and cover letters and conducted over 500 interviews.

Scott has a passion for solving complex problems and helping others learn. He lives in west suburban Chicago with his wife, Margie, and their three teenage boys.